The Book of Great

AMERICAN FIRECRACKERS

Johnny's Reflections

When July Fourth Comes roun',
my pa He gets things for us boys-
Firecrackers, rockets, tor-pe-does and things to make a noise.
He sez 'all patriots mus' show the'r patri'tism now,
But when we go to touch 'em off, he has to show us how.
My pa sets the crackers off, they go with great KA-POW!
An pa he sez "See, Johnnie boy, one day I'll show you how."
But ifin I go to light a fuse an pa sees what I'm at,
my pa he hollars "Hol' on there, son! You best let me do that."
When I grow up, my little boys C'n have a fireworks store.
an I won't never strike a match ner touch things off no more.
I'll jest set roun' an see the things explode and raise a row,
And I won't say, "Hol' on there, son, Best let me show you how."
— Baltimore Resident

Jack Nash

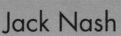

ESSEX SPECIALTY COMPANY, INC.
BERKELEY HEIGHTS, N.J.

ATOMIC BRAND
FLASH BANG
2 Inch
SALUTES
manufactured by
NORDLINGER-CHARLTON FIREWORKS CO.
CAUTION EXPLOSIVE

TORPEDOES
NEW JERSEY FIREWORKS MFG. CO. INC

The Book of Great

AMERICAN
FIRECRACKERS

Cherry Bombs, M-80s, Cannon Crackers, and More

Schiffer Publishing Ltd
4880 Lower Valley Road • Atglen, PA 19310

The formulas given in this publication are for reference only and are extremely dangerous. Only qualified persons with complete knowledge of pyrotechnics, pyrotechnic formulas and principles of explosives, and all related safety procedures necessary to handle these materials should even consider making any of the items described in this book. Furthermore, local, state, and federal laws give very stiff penalties for manufacture or possession of explosive devices. Do not risk serious injury or lengthy jail time: it is not worth it! If you would like to learn more about pyrotechnic chemistry, consider becoming a member of any of the fine national pyrotechnic organizations. The author and publisher take no responsibility for the use of any of the materials or methods described in this book, nor for the products thereof.

Type set in Bodoni Std, Flash & Futura Std.

ISBN: 978-0-7643-5142-6
Printed in China

Published by Schiffer Publishing, Ltd.
4880 Lower Valley Road
Atglen, PA 19310
Phone: (610) 593-1777; Fax: (610) 593-2002
E-mail: Info@schifferbooks.com
Web: www.schifferbooks.com

For our complete selection of fine books on this and related subjects, please visit our website at www.schifferbooks.com. You may also write for a free catalog.

Schiffer Publishing's titles are available at special discounts for bulk purchases for sales promotions or premiums. Special editions, including personalized covers, corporate imprints, and excerpts, can be created in large quantities for special needs. For more information, contact the publisher.

We are always looking for people to write books on new and related subjects. If you have an idea for a book, please contact us at proposals@schifferbooks.com.

Contents

Introduction

Just about everybody loves the 4th of July and the fireworks that accompany the celebration. Independence Day is an exclusively American celebration of freedom, liberty, and the pursuit of happiness, just as our founding **fathers** envisioned. Constitutionalist John Adams said of the 4th of July, "It ought to be solemnized with Pomp and Parade, with Shews [Shows], Games, Sports, Bells, Bonfires and Illuminations from one end of the continent to the other from this Time forward forever more." Surely by "illuminations" he meant the fireworks of the day. And as much as the meaning of freedom has changed from John Adams's day, when an American individual was truly free to do and say what he wanted—keeping within the boundaries of common sense of course—to the present day, so too are the 4th of Julys of today much different than the 4th of Julys of the days gone by.

Growing up in the 1950s, I was at the tail end of the era of the Great American Firecracker. Back then, for most young boys, the 4th of July was the best holiday ever! My friends and I would save our money for months in preparation, and talk and dream and scheme of acquiring the celebration item of choice for most young boys—the firecracker. But that was just the main classification in which lie many subspecies, and we knew them all by name, type, and manufacturer: Cherry Bombs, Silver Salutes, M-80s, Blockbusters, Ash Cans, Barrel Bombs, and Torpedoes, right down to imported Chinese "inch and a halfers" and lady fingers. Of course, the girls would have nothing to do with them; like fishin' worms and pet snakes, firecrackers were strictly a boy's obsession.

No matter how much my friends and I worked and saved and planned to get our grubby little hands on a decent supply of firecrackers for the 4th of July, we were always faced with the same daunting problem: locating a supplier. When it came to fireworks, growing up in the 1950s meant you lived in a divided America. Almost like the Civil War, the battle lines were drawn and the country was divided into states. There were firework states (Tennessee,

Ohio, Missouri, Oklahoma, South Carolina, Alabama, the Dakotas, and others), where you could buy any type of fireworks known to man legally. Cannon crackers, Roman candles, sky rockets, buzz bombs, aerial bombs…anything you could dream of or desire in the way of fireworks was readily available and sold everywhere from the corner fireworks stand to the local dime store, drug store, and grocery stores. I remember clearly my "first time." I was on a vacation to California with my parents. We stopped at a large grocery store in Missouri and I could not believe my eyes. There, among the cereal boxes and loaves of bread, were brightly colored skyrockets, boxes of Silver Salutes, and bricks of Chinese firecrackers; a world I never knew existed.

Then there were the rest of the states, like the one I lived in, Indiana. These were called "Safe and Sane" states. A Safe and Sane state was one where elderly ladies, over-protective mothers, and various other lobbies had seriously restricted or completely outlawed sales and the possession of fireworks altogether. In my home state of Indiana only four items were legal: sparklers, snakes, fountains, and caps; that was it. Anything that flew in the air, moved on the ground (or moved at all!), popped, exploded, or made noise was strictly illegal, and the heavy hand of the law and stiff penalties were usually enough to limit fearful firework lovers and dealers into compliance. Every year the local media would saturate our Indiana town with all the propaganda horror stories of deadly and destructive fireworks and the serious consequences of their sales and use. Blinded, limb-less children whose houses had burned to the ground and would live the rest of their lives in pain and torture from the use of fireworks and their consequences. Little did we know, for all the scare tactics, drama, and exaggeration, there was definitely a spark of truth to what they were telling us. But all we cared about was the fact that the establishment was depriving us kids of great fun and joy! So we contented ourselves to our sparklers and fountains for our 4th of July fireworks celebration, all the while pretending these "toys" were the real thing by squeezing every ounce of performance out of them with sheer ingenuity. Throwing a sparkler in the air became a skyrocket. If you laid a fountain on its side it would fly along the ground, and if you managed to stomp on it with the heel of your shoe it would explode like a firecracker. Oftentimes the grand finale of our display consisted of lighting as many sparklers as we could at one time and throwing them high into the air. If you got enough kids together this turned into a pretty impressive display.

But one had to question the rationale and logic of the laws in our state. A legal, lighted sparkler thrown high into the air versus an illegal bottle rocket. Sparklers burn hot; they are burning pieces of iron, virtually molten metal, and when you throw one in the air, it stays lit when it comes down. You can do this over and over before the sparkler is finally consumed, which lends plenty of opportunities for the lowly little sparkler to land most anywhere. In your sister's golden locks, on the family automobile, or as happened with my next door neighbor, in an evergreen tree, first setting the tree on fire and then spreading to the entire roof of the house before the firemen finally arrived to put it out. Not to mention all the inebriated fathers shooting their guns into the air in celebration; all those bullets had to land somewhere. Although it was rare for a falling bullet to hit someone, it did happen. On the other hand, a bottle rocket goes shooting skyward, gives a pop and a flash, and falls harmlessly to earth, spent and extinguished. Or you light a salute that goes off with the "KA-POW" of a shotgun, but no bullets fall to earth. So which is "Safe and Sane?" It was then I found the revelation the lawmakers had missed: "Safe and Sane" refers to the people who are using the fireworks and not the fireworks themselves. You can't legislate safe and sane, you can only educate people how to safely use fireworks, whether a Cherry Bomb or a sparkler.

None of this stopped any of us boys; we would figure out a way to get our firecrackers by hook or by crook, and we could outrun most anyone.

So we had several options for acquiring the coveted stash. The best was the family vacation. If your family went on a long trip anytime during the year, chances were good you would be going through a legal firework state at some point along the way. You would know immediately when you crossed that state line, because the highway would be lined with firework stands with names like "Loco Joe's Fireworks & Pecans" or "Crazy Bob's Fireworks"—even the "Stuckey's" chain got in on the action. This was the best way to stock up for the 4th, because you had the most variety to choose from and you got more for your money. All that competition meant lower prices. All you had to do was overcome a couple obstacles, like getting your dad, who was hell bent on driving 750 miles a day, to stop for you, and then convincing your mom you were old enough and responsible enough to buy a couple gross of M-80s or Cherry Bombs when she new they were illegal at home. Dad would usually side with you on that one because he also enjoyed setting off a few. This was also the best way because you could end up selling half of what you bought to your buddies,

A 1940s safe and sane public service sign warns of the dangers of playing with firecrackers. *Library of Congress*

thereby getting yours for free. Of course, this also worked in reverse: if one of your buddies went on vacation and you didn't it kind of evened out.

If you were a kid growing up in the 1950s and your parents took you on a vacation either west to California or south to Florida, you had to go past a seemingly endless number of firework stands and signs. This is a typical flyer from a "legal" fireworks state c. 1950.

There were several other much riskier and more expensive methods we used if we could not purchase our firecrackers legally out of state. Out of town vagabonds who worked out of their car would often set up small stands on the corner of the highway. On the tables would be all the typical legal stuff—sparklers and snakes—but you never knew what they had in the trunk of the car that was usually parked a block away. Indiana had very harsh laws back then: one dealer from Tennessee got two years in jail for selling cherry bombs out of his trunk, so this was serious business. They wouldn't sell to you right away; they had to check you out first and make sure you weren't a snitch. Sometimes it could take a couple trips back and forth to the stand, repeatedly asking for the "good stuff" over and over before they would relent and let you see inside the trunk and sell you some very expensive cherry bombs or M-80s. The last resort was relying on the neighborhood adults. Since illegal fireworks were available in the neighboring state of Ohio, every year certain groups of adults would make the 200-mile trip and risk the stiff penalties to purchase full displays. They believed it was their constitutional right to celebrate the 4th with the fireworks of their choosing, so they would gather—usually at some secluded place along the St. Joe River, where you could see a cop car from a mile away—and shoot off their illegal display. Any sign of the law and people would disburse into the woods like rabbits, only to reappear when the coast was clear. Of course this attracted all the young boys in town. We would watch the displays with great enthusiasm and fascination while the adults guzzled beer and hooted and hollered. And maybe, just maybe we could talk somebody into selling us a pack of firecrackers or a couple Cherry Bombs, or maybe at least let us light one. What a thrill. Then bright and early the next morning, we would return to the scene of the crime to collect all the leftover debris: boxes, labels, and especially duds and misfires, were great treasures. If you were an American boy growing up after WWII, your absolute favorite 4th of July celebration item was the firecracker,

9

From the late 1800s through the 1930s, the fireworks business was steadily supported by America's love of firecrackers. While firecrackers had long ago been established as the celebratory item of choice for young boys on the 4th of July, in the southern US, it was a tradition to use firecrackers to celebrate Christmas. In fact, more firecrackers were sold in the southern states at Christmas time than any other time of the year. This seems to be exclusively a southern tradition that may have started during the Civil War. In the South, it was traditional to give firecrackers and other gifts in observance of the Christmas holiday and indeed, most young boys looked forward to receiving firecrackers for Christmas more than toys or any other gift.

and the bigger the better. Living in a "safe and sane" state only made one more determined to acquire them. . .the coveted big American firecrackers.

Over the years, many fine books have been written about all manner of fireworks manufacture, history, and collecting. Most of the books dealing with pyrobilia deal with Chinese firecrackers, and with good reason. Of all the fireworks in the world, Chinese firecrackers have the most beautiful and diverse labels; their vast array, rarity, and eye-popping designs make for a great collecting hobby and are no doubt the most popular pursuit among pyrobilia collectors. This book is probably the first dealing solely with Great American Firecrackers from their inception into American celebrations—replacing dangerous celebratory gun and cannon fire—until the final federal ban with the Child Protection Act of 1966, a time when hundreds of American companies produced all manner of salutes and firecrackers, up to a whopping fifteen inch long by two inch diameter. After WWII, most ammunition companies turned to making fireworks for the civilian market. Other manufacturers sprang up overnight and blew themselves away just as fast. Of all American-made fireworks, large firecrackers, salutes, and cherry bombs were the easiest and cheapest to make, were the most popular with consumers, and yielded the highest profit. Competition was stiff, but business was booming. Sadly, it is also true that of all fireworks made, nothing was more detrimental to the fireworks trade than large firecrackers. Every 4th of July hundreds, if not thousands, of people were seriously injured, maimed, or blinded, most often due

to ignorance, like putting them under tin cans, throwing them at unsuspecting persons, or holding them after lighting until the last possible moment in some twisted attempt to prove their manhood. These then are the stories and products from the era of the "Great American Firecracker"—the most dangerous era in American fireworks history.

Chapter 1

A Brief History of the Firecracker

It is widely believed the very first firecrackers of sorts came about as a result of natural materials reacting to early man's first real technological breakthrough, the discovery of fire. We have all had the experience of sitting around a campfire and the crackling, hissing, and popping of the wood as it burns. Some woods pop louder than others, and at times can even produce a loud and frightening bang that fills the air with sparks as a result of tiny, airtight chambers in the wood or plant that build up pressure in the heat of the fire until the hot gasses break through the chamber, causing varying degrees of explosions. Perfection of these airtight chambers in the form of a plant are found in bamboo. Bamboo is a very unique plant that is actually a member of the grass family. It is the fastest growing plant on earth. Bamboo's unique hollow, segmented construction, with its very strong, fibrous wall, makes it the perfect exploding plant, as the people who first put it on a campfire would so abruptly discover. It is believed the Chinese were the first to discover the explosive power of bamboo, well before they invented gunpowder. The Chinese found that sealed sections of green bamboo soaked in water (so as not to burn through the outer wall before the interior gasses could heat up) that were then thrown into an open fire would explode with a very loud report indeed. The Chinese soon made use of this knowledge to scare away enemies, animals, and evil spirits, and in doing so most likely invented the very first firecracker—it came from the fire and it cracked.

Although there is some debate as to by whom and when gunpowder was first discovered, the overwhelming academic consensus is that it was discovered by

Chinese alchemists, most likely completely by accident around the eleventh century. Gunpowder is included as one of the four great Chinese inventions; the other three are the compass, paper making, and printing. There seems to be a misconception among pyrotechnic devotees that the Chinese invented gunpowder expressly for the purpose of making fireworks. While this is quite the romantic notion, it is most likely not the case. Unfortunately, as with most great discoveries and inventions, military application was probably the foremost consideration of this amazing new discovery. Indeed,

Bamboo plant showing sealed section chambers.

the earliest known recorded formula dates back to approximately 1040. This was not the explosive gunpowder we know of today, but a highly flammable powder that was used in combination with bamboo poles as "fire lances" or flame throwers. These were weapons that used hollow bamboo poles filled with a type of saltpeter powder formulation to fire small projectiles. Also pots of burning powder could be dumped down upon enemies from high places. The Chinese invented fireworks in the tenth century as a means to chase away evil spirits. Other weapons were developed and experimentation with the general gunpowder formula continued until its full explosive nature was realized about the middle of the twelfth century, with about eight different formulas being used for different applications. Over 200 years in the making, finally the main explosive formula of 75% saltpeter, 15% charcoal, and 10% sulfur—basically the same as modern gunpowder—was finally discovered. The Chinese soon learned that filling vessels of iron, bamboo, and clay with the explosive powder made a formidable and fearsome weapon, not so much for its lethality, but because it gave them the ability to terrify and intimidate the enemy. So the Chinese came to create lightning and thunder, and the groundwork for the modern firecracker was laid. Instead of bamboo, stiff paper was used with a charge of "black" powder and a fuse that could be timed.

The Chinese used brilliant full-colored artwork to create labels for their firecrackers. Since without the labels all Chinese firecrackers looked the same, this greatly helped sales—an idea American manufacturers would adapt for their products.

So how exactly is a traditional Chinese firecracker made and how does it work? In a nutshell, the whole procedure from beginning to end goes something like this: Because of the dangerous nature of the black powder, it was mixed in small batches as needed in storage sheds away from the main assembly areas and then brought in. Then a piece of paper about one-third inch wide by fourteen inches long is laid out on a table, onto which a line of black powder is spread in the center with a small tube. This is then twisted up and secured with wheat paste and becomes the fuse. The firecracker tubes are made with a cheap grade of straw paper that is wrapped around a metal forming rod, tightened with a special tool, glued with wheat paste, and allowed to dry in the sun. The firecracker tubes are then gathered in bundles of hundreds and securely tied together with string. Clay powder is then spread over the bottoms of the tubes and consolidated with a hammer and punch, thereby plugging one end of the tube. Black powder is added and a fuse is inserted in each firecracker, and the end is then crimped with a dull nail or punch and a hammer. The finished firecrackers are braided into various-sized packs (usually 16, 32, 50, 100, and larger rolls or coils) and wrapped in brightly colored cellophane. A brand label is then added to each pack and the packs are consolidated into larger packages known as bricks. The finished firecrackers are shipped to their final destination and purchased by the end user. The firecrackers are then unwrapped and either lit one at a time by upbraiding the string or the entire string is fired. The explosion is caused mainly by the saltpeter, which provides its own source of oxygen.

Because it contains a large amount of oxygen, saltpeter can burn even in the vacuum of space, which is why it can also burn in a sealed tube. Sulfur acts as a combustion enhancer, lowering the high burning point of the saltpeter to about 500 degrees and causing a chemical reaction, liquefying the mixture and raising the temperature to around 625 degrees. The charcoal acts as a fuel and is instantly oxidized in a reaction, further raising the temperature to about 7,000 degrees. The resulting chemical reaction converts the chemicals into carbon and sulfide gases to about 3,000% of the original mass of the powder, causing great pressure on the walls of the paper container that cannot contain the expanding gasses (much like the bamboo on the campfire) and explodes with a loud and powerful noise. So there you have it. From creation to explosion, the firecracker is born.

Trade was rapidly developing between countries and continents. China and Asia were especially popular trade partners with Italy and Europe because of the desirability of their spices, silk fabrics, and other goods unique to China at the time. Firecrackers and black powder were among the items brought to Europe from China. It has been recorded that the famous explorer Marco Polo, who first opened the trade routes to China, brought a supply of black powder ingredients and Chinese firecrackers and rockets back to his native Italy in 1295. Perhaps in a sudden fit of modern salesmanship, he is quoted as describing them with great exaggeration, stating, "The firecrackers burn with such a dreadful noise that they can be heard for 10 miles in the night and anyone hearing this could die." The Italians soon took the newfound knowledge of black powder and fireworks and turned it into a world class art form. They were most likely the first to use black powder to produce the modern aerial "shell" type firework that is the heart of the modern fireworks display we know today.

Black powder and firecrackers soon spread to all of Europe. They were first used in England in 1486, at the marriage of King Edward VII. By the mid-1600s, England's King Charles II had a division of his military trained expressly for handling and exploding firecrackers and fireworks. The use of firecrackers and fireworks became commonplace for England's royalty and well-to-do for celebration, novelty, and amusement. Once different countries had firecrackers and the raw materials and chemicals to make their own, many improvements, experiments, inventions, and innovations began to appear, including the invention that would change the world: the gun. But by and large, nobody could improve on the original Chinese firecracker. Most all firecrackers made and used still came from China for several reasons: they required great skill to produce in great quantities; and they were extremely labor intensive, making them expensive to produce in more developed countries like England, Italy, and Spain. The Chinese had the knowledge, history, expertise, cheap labor, and the skilled workers to produce firecrackers in mass quantities, and they did it better than anybody else could. Making firecrackers in a Chinese firecracker factory was terrible work: the hours were long, the conditions were horrid, and the pay was even worse. Skilled firecracker makers would have a quota that often required them to work sixteen hours a day and seven days a week, for which they got

The Chinese used brilliant full-colored artwork to create labels for their firecrackers. Since without the labels all Chinese firecrackers looked the same, this greatly helped sales, an idea American manufacturers would adapt for their products. Because of the great selection and rarity of certain labels, Chinese firecracker labels are the most sought after items among pyrobilia collectors.

paid five to ten cents. Firecrackers were usually made by whole Chinese families, with the family members involved in every step of the process, including selling them to the public or exporters. Often times the women and children of the family would work for no pay at all, with only the privilege of being provided for by the family trade as their reward. The production and business of firecracker making in China remained basically the same for more than 400 years. All of this set the stage for the firecracker's debut in the "new world." The firecracker was ready for America, but was America ready for the firecracker? Oh yeah!

Chapter 2

The Firecracker Comes to America

Firecrackers were widely used in most of the civilized world by the time the first English settlers reached the shores of the New World, and it is a sure bet they brought them with them. By the time the settlers arrived in America, black powder was a necessary commodity in the vast new wilderness. Firecrackers were used to celebrate special occasions, to scare away animals and Native Americans, and were still believed to scare away evil spirits. Firecrackers and fireworks in general were so widely used and misused that the first of what must have been numerous bans in America over the years was established as early as 1731. By the Revolutionary War, firecrackers were very much a part of special celebrations. Although fireworks were used to celebrate even before the signing of the Declaration of Independence on July 4, 1776, they forever became associated with that holiday thereafter. One of the main reasons firecrackers were used for celebrations was they replaced the widely held practice of shooting guns into the air and other not-so-safe noise-making practices, such as the anvil shoot, wherein two very heavy anvils were placed one inverted on top of the other with a bag of black powder in between; when a fuse was lit, it would explode the bag of powder with a great "KA-BOOM," sending a heavy anvil hurling high into the air. It was very important to watch the skies for falling anvils when doing this, lest they land squarely on your head. And if many teams of fathers and sons were doing this together in a field, it could get very confusing and dangerous as to when there was an anvil on the fall or not. Another popular noisemaker was the cannon. These came in all shapes and sizes, from the full-scale used in warfare all the way down to

one a boy could carry in his pocket. All these cannons had one thing in common: the barrels were all made of cast iron, which is strong yet brittle. Every cannon had a certain amount of powder it could fire reasonably safely, but in pursuit of an increasingly louder bang they were inevitably overfilled, creating devastating, shrapnel-producing bombs that would take down anything in the immediate area. Every year, many a young boy would be killed or seriously injured not following directions and warnings and putting too large a powder load into his toy cannon. Compared to some of these dangerous celebratory practices, firecrackers became a relatively safe alternative. Firecrackers could simulate gunfire and cannon fire, and to this day it is hard to distinguish the sound of one from the other. What better way to celebrate our freedom on this, the most joyous and liberating of all American holidays, than by the use of fireworks and toy cannon fire?

On July 3, 1776—before the Declaration was even signed—John Adams envisioned the importance of the document when he wrote to his wife, "The day will be the most memorable in the history of America. I am apt to believe that it will be celebrated by succeeding generations as the great anniversary festival." Indeed, with pomp and parade and bountiful fireworks, the tradition of celebrating the greatest of American holidays was established. In that same spirit, many more patriotic events and spectacles were celebrated with firecrackers and fireworks. In 1789, the inauguration of America's first president, George Washington, was celebrated with the most beautiful of firework displays. Soon politicians of all sorts would use firecrackers and fireworks to attract crowds and use the emotion and sense of patriotism associated with previous ceremonies to gain favor with constituents.

Although the Chinese were still making practically all of the firecrackers being consumed by Americans, American ingenuity was soon to bring itself to the industry in a big way. The firecracker, which had basically remained the same for 600 years, was about to go through the most dramatic and varied transformation one could imagine, and those changes were about to come fast and furious, in the true spirit of American entrepreneurship. First on the agenda was to try and produce the firecrackers here in America, which had not been attempted before. The market for firecrackers and fireworks of all types was growing fast, but the transportation fees involved in importing them from China was making them cost prohibitive, especially after the government put a 200% import tariff on imported firecrackers in the 1890s. Up to this point, it was not worth the effort to make them in America because the Chinese product was of good quality and very inexpensive, even taking the importing costs into consideration.

Eventually, an American named Gerhard opened America's first firecracker factory in 1894, in the town of Greenville, New Jersey. At last, America's first firecracker factory! But it was not to be and Mr. Gerhard's factory shut down as fast as it opened. Mr. Gerhard learned there was just no way to compete with the Chinese and their cheap labor and high productivity, not to mention centuries of firecracker manufacturing experience. In America it has always been about the dollar, so where the Chinese could produce endless

Gunpowder was vital to the survival of the early settlers in America. The first recorded gunpowder mill in America was built in Milton, Massachusetts. If not for the fact that by 1775 America had set up its own powder mills, the Revolutionary War may have been lost. This hand bill advertising gunpowder for sale from one of America's early mills details the different types of powder made by the company.

supplies of firecrackers at little cost, Mr. Gerhard could only produce half as many and at twice the cost. There was just no way American companies could compete with the 600-year-old firecracker-making tradition. Once that lesson was learned, it was onward to the American way of doing things: innovation, invention, technology, novelty, advertising, packaging, and promotion were what American businessmen did best. Leave the old behind and create the new! The demand for the product was there, and America could show the world how it was done.

The timing was right for a change; America was going crazy with new ideas and advancements and China had become bogged down in political revolution and upheaval. Fireworks and firecrackers were so popular the Chinese product could no longer meet worldwide demand. American firecracker and fireworks companies emerged overnight, each innovating, creating, and competing to feed the public's great demand.

The first really great technological advance that made manufacturing possible in America was to come to the very heart and soul of the firecracker—the powder. Gunpowder had been in existence for centuries, with very little changes to its formulation, but a new powder was about to be adapted for use in another invention that had created a whole new industry—the camera.

The photograph was exciting and all the rage in turn-of-the-century America. At last, images could be captured and saved without having an artist paint a subject. But all photography depends on light, and in the early days it took great amounts of light and long exposures to produce results. To fulfill the desire for brilliant bright light available on demand, in 1894, Alexander Hensley invented a new chemical mixture he called photographic flash-light compound. This was a mixture of nitrate, phosphorus, and magnesium that could be easily ignited and produced a flash of brilliant light upon ignition. As it turned out, the new "flash powder" was also a wonderful new explosive when lightly contained. No longer was a thick-walled and tightly sealed tube required for an explosion to occur. It is believed the Germans were the first to experiment with this new formula as it was applied to fireworks. In 1899, a German scientist named Alfone Bujard wrote the first modern book on firework chemistry, *The Art of Fireworks*, in which he described new formulations of black powder with the addition of metal powders such as aluminum and magnesium for ease of ignition and incredible brightness. After many centuries, this new discovery was about to change the whole world of the firecracker. This new formula was much more explosive than black powder, making it much more sensitive to shock, friction, and static electricity; a new and exciting world of firecrackers was about to be born, as well as the long and dangerous history of factory accidents and explosions that seemed to come with the new explosive powder.

This was the start of the "bigger is better" principle that has long been a part of American ideology. With the introduction of the new and bigger "flash powder"-based firecracker, Americans were rapidly losing interest in the common Chinese firecracker, which had become boring and commonplace. New firework companies were springing up from coast to coast, and although all fireworks sold well, by far the largest profits and greatest

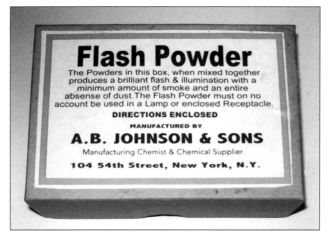

With the invention of photography came the need for an "on demand" source of bright light to facilitate proper exposure of the film. This was accomplished with the use of a magnesium-based powder. This new formula was soon adopted by the American firecracker industry.

sales would come from the big salute-type firecracker. All of these factors gave birth to the era of the Great American Firecracker, and business was literally booming! It seemed as though virtually every firecracker manufacturer blew itself up sooner or later, sometimes with extremely devastating and tragic results. The new powders were way more sensitive to handle and many times safety concerns were overlooked to meet production quotas. And if it wasn't the factories blowing up, it was the retailers or consumers. Every year hundreds of people would be killed or injured using large firecrackers, and more often the casualties were children. Some states and communities tried hard to regulate the sale and use of firecrackers, but all one had to do was travel to a place not far away to purchase all the firecrackers one desired, in all shapes, sizes, and brands, and anybody could afford them, as they were boxed in various quantities from three to a gross (144).

Chapter 3
American Firecrackers: Types, Sizes & Innovations

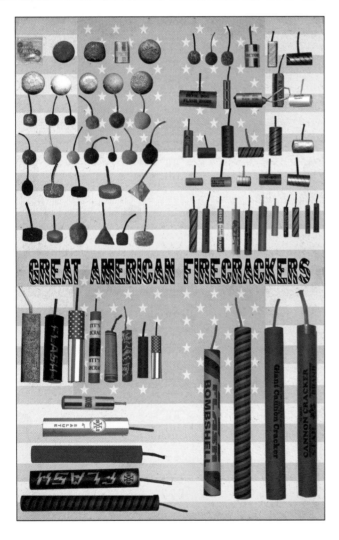

public, and so were innovations in safety and performance.

It is hard to fathom today, but up until 1912, there were places in America you could legally purchase and freely set off firecrackers up to thirteen inches long and two inches in diameter. In his book that has become the pyrotechnic bible and probably the best book on the manufacture of fireworks ever written, *The Dictionary and Manual of Fireworks*, author George Wiengart published a chart standardizing the various sizes of salutes and firecrackers for commercial production and sale. The smaller crackers (up to about three inches) were usually referred to as "salutes," while the bigger ones were known as "cannon crackers." After 1912, salutes were limited in size to five inches long by ¾ inch diameter—still a very big and powerful firecracker.

The following are standard salute sizes:

NUMBER	LENGTH	BORE	NO. IN BOX	BOXES IN CASE
1	2 in.	5/16 in.	100	20
2	3 in.	5/16 in.	50	25
3	3½ in.	3/8 in.	15	100
4	4 in.	7/16 in.	30	20
5	5 in.	½ in.	20	20
7	6½ in.	5/8 in.	10	20
9	8 in.	¾ in.	5	20
10	9½ in.	7/8 in.	3	20
12	10½ in.	1 in.	2	20
15	13 in.	1¾ in.		25

As supply and demand for large American firecrackers went up, up, up, so too did the competition for the consumer dollar. In an attempt to capture more of the expanding market, new styles, types, and sizes of salutes were being introduced to the hungry

Although there was an attempt to standardize sizes, there was no consistency from manufacturer to manufacturer as to how much powder or the type of powder that was contained in each salute. Generally speaking, the smaller salutes used a flash powder formula that varied from one manufacturer to the next, and the larger salutes still used black powder. Black powder was cheaper and more plentiful, but not as sensitive as the flash compositions. Because of this, cannon crackers made with black powder required a stout, tightly sealed case to build up enough pressure for a decent explosion. Early flash composition was made with chlorate of potash (potassium chlorate), and although it was very sensitive and dangerous to use, it was the composition of choice with the early manufacturers. It was not until T. G. Hitt experimented with the sensitivity issue that flash formulas became relatively safe to use (see chapter 5). Each company had its own formula of powder, and each one tried to add a special effect, squeeze out more bang for the buck, or add some unique quality to their product. Some would add more aluminum or magnesium for greater flash. Antimony trisulphide could be substituted for sulphur, or flake aluminum could be added for electric effect. The Kent Manufacturing Company of Chestertown, Massachusetts, confounded the competition briefly (until someone finally dissected one of their cherry bombs) by adding a colored "star," like those used in aerial shells, to the flash charge; this added a bit of color to the flash as the cherry bomb went off. But because of the lack of any standardization of the explosive powder in each salute, it was impossible for the consumer to know what he was getting when it came to the "bang factor." For example, one manufacturer's two-inch salute could contain four grams of flash powder while another might contain twelve grams, so one two-inch salute would be much louder than another. This would eventually cause customers to develop a loyalty to a certain brand that would spill over into the sales of other items in their firework line. Early on, the Unexcelled Manufacturing Company of New York established itself as one of the best for quality and variety. Until the 1930s, the Unexcelled Company was the biggest manufacturer of large firecrackers in the country. They made highly rated salutes and cannon crackers of every size and shape and packaged them in fanciful boxes in small to large quantities, trying to cover all corners of the market.

In the beginning, not much attention was paid to the finishing or packaging of salutes and crackers; salutes were rather plain, packaged in boxes with plain block letters. But as competition increased, American manufacturers borrowed from the Chinese and began to wrap individual salutes with brightly colored paper and attractively designed artwork. This would slowly but eventually evolve into warning labels on several sides of the boxes and also on the crackers themselves, ending up as one big warning. If you saw a box of salutes in the mid-1960s, you would think you had a box of "DO NOT HOLD IN HAND," but early on there was not a warning statement in sight on boxes of salutes.

While the invention of photoflash powder gave rise to the development of the Chinese firecracker's evolution into the American salute, it also allowed for the form of the firecracker container itself to be changed. The new photoflash formulas were extremely powerful and very sensitive. Salutes no longer had to be made with strong tubes with heavy-end plugs. Where black powder was slow burning and needed to be tightly contained to build up enough pressure to explode, the photoflash powders burned almost instantaneously. A salute could be produced with flash powder using just a couple turns of paper, opening the door for the creation of many different shapes of salutes, most of which were made from formed paper, sawdust, and glue, such as "barrel bombs" (shaped like whiskey barrels), pyramid-shaped salutes, and cube- or square-shaped salutes. Probably the most popular firecracker of all time is the Cherry Bomb or Globe Salute. If a container could be made of paper or any other material that did not produce much shrapnel, it could be made into a salute.

The Cherry Bomb (also called the Globe Salute, Kraft Salute, or Bangarang) first appeared in America in the late 1920s. It is unclear exactly who invented it. A story in an early 1930s edition of the *New York Times* about a United States Senate subcommittee on juvenile delinquency credits the invention of the Cherry Bomb to Bernard J. Semel. He does hold a patent for this type of device, but there are several other patents by various inventors for round or globe salutes that started appearing between 1929 and 1932, so it is hard to tell who was the first to invent the Cherry Bomb. A patent filed in January 1929 by Alberto Cimorosi seems to be the first time anyone suggested a molded spherical firecracker case resembling the modern form of the Cherry Bomb we knew in later years. It was usually made by filling a set of nesting cardboard cups with flash powder, covering one cup with the other inverted one. The assembled set of cups was then coated with a thick mixture of glue (usually sodium silicate, also known as water glass) and sawdust to form a very hard shell. A hole was then poked in it and the fuse glued in place. This process was also used to form other shapes, such as the barrel bomb and pyramid. Cherry Bombs started out as globe salutes and came in all different sizes and many assorted colors, until someone noticed a red sphere with a green fuse gave the globe salute the appearance of a cherry and the new nickname Cherry Bomb was born.

The popularity of the Cherry Bomb skyrocketed, exceeding sales of ordinary salutes. Soon every manufacturer was making their own brand of Cherry Bomb or globe salute. Once again, there was a race to see who could make the better product the fastest. Cherry Bombs were by nature harder to make than your standard tube salute; they were round, making them roll around on workspaces and hard to handle. They required extra finishing and molding to get the glue and sawdust wall that was sometimes up to half an inch thick. To achieve this thickness, sometimes the Cherry Bombs would have to be put through the coating process two to three times, with drying time in between. Every manufacturer had a secret process to achieve the end result.

Although some companies tried early on to produce Cherry Bombs using standard black powder, the results were not very satisfactory; the potassium perchlorate, aluminum, and sulphur flash powder worked much better. Each manufacturer had their own special powder recipe and there were hundreds of variations by the 1940s. Formulas were developed to meet the needs of the manufacturers with many precise considerations in mind, such as thickness of the container wall, sensitivity in mixing and detonation, availability and cost of ingredients, shelf life, how much powder could be mixed at one time, etc. Much trial and error in the formulation of the explosive power was done to get the right mixture for the job. Until T. G. Hitt patented his safer version of flash powder, manufacturers were still using variations of the potassium chlorate mixture, but by this time most manufactures were at least aware of the extreme and dangerous nature of the potassium chlorate formulas and that they should be avoided if possible.

The makers of American salutes would try most anything to make their products stand out from the pack. Manufacturers who skimped on the amount of

Kent Cherry Flash Salutes was probably the best selling brand of Cherry Bombs of all time. Popular with "juvenile delinquents" as stated in a Senate subcommittee in the 1950s, it is probably responsible for more broken commodes and mailboxes than any other single cause.

powder they put into their salutes would have to count on their discounted price, first-time buyers, or other name brands selling out fast at the retail level to sell their product. Some things worked and some didn't; pyramid salutes proved too hard to make and faded fast. One manufacturer glued printed animal die cuts to their salutes, naming them "Animal Crackers." It seems there was not a great demand from people wanting to see pictures of animals blown up, resulting in a short run. One very successful marketing move was simple: just by wrapping the 1½-inch case in silver paper with "Do Not Hold in Hand" printed in a never-ending spiral around the tube and moving the fuse from the end to the side produced what was probably the second most popular salute ever made, the Silver Salute.

Then there was the M-80. Originally made by firework makers under contract to the United States military, the M-80—whose name was basically a military stock or item number: M for military and 80 the number of grains of powder (approximately five grams)—was used to simulate gunfire during military basic training. It originally had a plain tan casing when made for the military, but soon after WWII was sold as surplus and eventually adapted for civilian sales. With a make-over and a bright red wrap printed with a big "M-80, Do Not Hold in Hand," the M-80 became a huge seller and rounded out the top three salutes (Cherry Bomb, Silver Salute, and the M-80).

Another popular type of firecracker was the torpedo or impact firecracker—much like the salutes but in a class by themselves. These made just as big a bang by

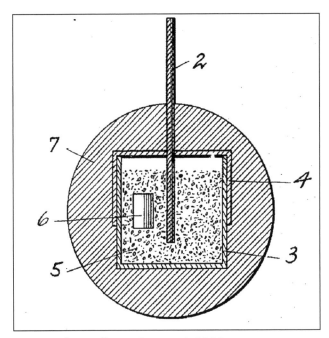

Diagram from Alberto Cimorosi's 1929 patent #1783999, showing how a cherry bomb is constructed. Cimorosi's patent seems to be the first time anyone considered a round salute. Notice the single "star" as made popular with the Kent brand cherry bomb. The cherry bomb was America's best selling and most infamous salute.

Rare 1930s photo showing a man making cherry bombs. To get a bigger bang out of the cherry bomb, the powder, which is in a flimsy paper cup, is confined more tightly by dipping the cracker repeatedly in silica gel and rolling it in sawdust. The rotating, cement-mixer-type drum in the background does this coating.

just throwing them down—no fire or fuse needed. Many of the patents, indeed most, related to Cherry Bombs or what I call shaped salutes also applied to toy torpedo designs. Torpedoes are basically fuseless salutes filled with impact-sensitive explosives and, most often, some fine gravel that promotes the generation of friction. Torpedoes were designed to detonate by throwing them down and striking a hard surface, initiating the explosion. Since the only real difference between a Cherry Bomb and a Globe Torpedo is the charge inside and lack of a fuse on the torpedo, new designs were pretty much interchangeable. Torpedoes were a very popular form of firecracker in the early twentieth century. They were sold in various sizes and types, some of which were every bit as powerful as any salutes. Torpedoes were much more dangerous than salutes because they produced a lot of shrapnel. Early explosive-powder torpedo formulas contained fulminates of metals such as mercury fulminate and silver fulminate. In George Weingart's 1937 book *Pyrotechnics*, he describes the making of silver fulminate using a common silver dollar. A very dangerous procedure indeed—you might as well try to make nitroglycerin! These explosive

compounds were very sensitive to friction and static electricity and heat and were very dangerous. They could only be mixed in very small, usually wet batches. They were also highly poisonous. Safer, less sensitive mixtures were later used, but the very nature of the torpedo device was always inherently dangerous. The outer coating was made of sodium silicate and sawdust or hardened clay that produced shards of sharp, hard, and almost glass-like shrapnel that flew with explosive velocity in all directions when a torpedo was detonated. To top it off, torpedoes were usually round and finished off in brightly colored paper and packaged in fancy boxes, making them particularly attractive to young children, who often mistook them for candy.

Twentieth-century firework companies realized they were making and selling very dangerous products, but with the handsome profits that could be made, they would deny the dangerous nature of their products and fight tooth and nail to keep them on the market. After years of mounting injuries and deaths—not only from the use of the products but also from disastrous factory explosions—the fireworks industry lost its battle to try and keep their most dangerous product—torpedoes—on the market. They were outlawed nationwide in the '50s, although you could still purchase a much smaller version called a "cracker ball." These were about as loud as a small Chinese firecracker. The "candy" problem still existed though, because these too were finished in brightly colored paper and small children tried to eat them, causing serious injury. A very stripped-down version of the torpedo still popular with children today is sold as Snap N' Pops or Pop Its, or other brand names, though they barely make a noise at all.

There were basically three types of torpedoes: the globe torpedo, the Japanese torpedo, and a specialty device used widely in the railroad industry known as the railway torpedo. The most popular by far was the globe torpedo. This was a round ball made of clay, paper maché, or glue and sawdust, much like a fuseless cherry bomb. They ranged in size from ¾ of an inch to about two inches. Although many variations of explosive formulas were used, the one below is typical of early torpedo chemistry for those not containing fulminates and comes from an 1867 clay torpedo patent by Charles Nelson:

Potassium Chlorate - 6 parts
Red Phosphorus - 6 parts
Sulphur - 3 parts
Powdered Chalk - 3 parts

Charles Nelson's torpedo patent was pretty simple. It consisted of a molded, solid clay ball with a hole extending halfway through in which the explosive could be placed and then sealed with the same type of clay. This effectively set the charge in the middle of the ball and also made the ball uniform, without a trace as to where the charge had been introduced. Nelson also gives directions in his patent as to the composition of the clay mixture to be used to facilitate strength; enough to be handled, but soft enough to break into dust and small pieces when detonated. This type of torpedo did throw off a lot of shrapnel and could not be stored for any extended period of time, as the clay would dry out and fall apart.

The Japanese torpedo is a relative of the cap used in toy cap guns and other toys. Caps were just small versions of impact firecrackers. Any young boy that played with a cap gun would sooner or later get around to hitting a whole roll of caps with a hammer on a hard

A popular 1950s version of the torpedo was named the "Cracker Ball" because of its similarity in sound to a 1½-inch firecracker. Their bright colors and twelve-per-bag packaging made them appealing to very young children who would often eat them with great consequence.

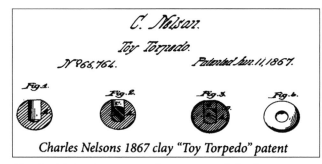

Charles Nelsons 1867 clay "Toy Torpedo" patent

Charles Nelson's toy torpedo was one of the first patents for an "impact" firecracker. It was simply a clay ball with a sensitive explosive charge at its center. It most likely produced a dangerous amount of shrapnel.

surface for a big bang. This is basically the effect you would get with a Japanese torpedo. This type of torpedo was much less sensitive than the globe torpedo and took a great deal of force to explode. Construction of a Japanese torpedo generally consisted of a specially made, extra-large paper cap situated in the center of a globe made of paper or clay, with the rest of the void filled with sand or fine gravel. The basic formula for the cap's composition was red phosphorus and potassium chlorate with a bit of sulphur and chalk. This was also a very dangerous composition to make due to the very nature of making an explosive mixture whose most important quality was to be sensitive to shock.

Although not an "entertainment" firecracker, the railway torpedo was directly related to the toy torpedo. It served an important purpose and was used for a specific function in the railway business. Large, puck-shaped torpedoes were fitted on the bottom with two lead strips that could be bent over a railroad rail, holding it in place anywhere along the railroad track. When run over by a train they would detonate and could be used

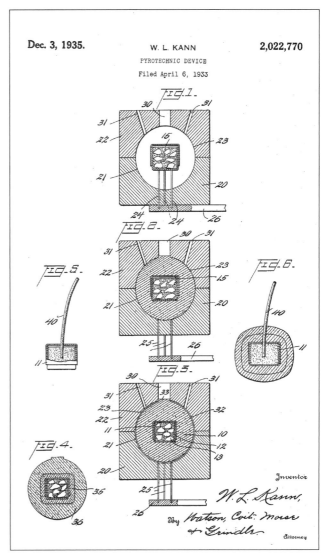

William Gehrig's "repeating torpedo" was basically a sheet of "caps" like those used in a toy cap gun, wrapped around a solid object such as a stone. Once impacted, the small explosions would move to the surrounding chemical deposits, causing them to detonate in repeating fashion.

William Kann's complicated apparatus for making a perfectly round cherry bomb. It is unknown if this device was ever used in mass production, but because of its intricacies it is doubtful.

to tell the engineer to stop, or give information about where the front or rear of the train was on the track. These were usually put on the railroad tracks by the flagman.

A few other inventions related to the variation and production of cherry bombs and torpedoes are worthy of note. A very interesting version of the torpedo was patented by W. F. Gehrig in 1925. What makes this version so interesting is that it did not explode just once, but many times, and was called a repeating torpedo by its inventor. Although it was a very ingenious and novel pyrotechnic invention, as with most of these highly unusual items, it was probably never actually manufactured. Indeed, no example is known to exist. W. F. Gehrig's repeating torpedo was accomplished by

placing many dabs of a special Japanese torpedo-type composition on squares of paper. This was then wrapped around a solid internal globe (the inventor suggests either a stone or a marble). It was finished off with an attractive colored-paper outer wrapper. When the torpedo was thrown down on a hard surface, the percussion would set off one of the dabs of composition, which in turn would set off the rest of the dabs, causing many successive explosions.

Those who are familiar with cherry bomb and torpedo construction are probably familiar with the cup set method of manufacture (where two paper cups are filled with powder and then dipped in some type of sealing composition) as being the most common. Upon inspection, this type of cherry bomb is easy to distinguish because it is not perfectly round; they appear more tubular or "hat box" shaped. This type was most common because of the ease of making them, but there were other types of cherry bombs and torpedoes that were perfectly formed globes, with the wall of the device uniform in thickness around the explosive charge in the center. The early clay-based casings were one way to make perfectly round globes, but these were somewhat fragile and had a very limited shelf life due to the drying and eventual disintegration of the clay. Much later, in the 1950s, two-piece plastic cherry bomb cases would be used to make the perfectly round plastic cherry bomb and were notorious for the plastic shrapnel they produced. In what must have been an aesthetic pursuit to make a perfectly round cherry bomb, several other inventors attempted various methods of forming and filling perfectly round globes for either cherry bombs or globe torpedoes, so one machine set-up served two purposes, producing two different products dependent on what formula was put inside each.

W. L. Kann's pyrotechnic device works basically like this: Fig. 1 shows a two-part spherical plaster mold inside which is a cup set containing an explosive charge (could be for either a cherry bomb or a torpedo) that is held in place dead center by three small nail-like rods attached to a small board or lever at the bottom that extend upward through the mold. The mold has air vents, allowing for the release of trapped air. In Fig. 2 a composition is then injected or poured into the mold through the hole in the top until the mold is completely filled and the explosive container is embedded into the center of the mixture. Fig 3. shows that at some point the mixture begins to solidify but is still significantly fluid, and the three rods supporting the explosive cup are removed by means of the lever at the bottom. This allows the three holes in the bottom of the shell casting to close up. The whole object is then allowed to solidify completely. When the mold is opened a perfectly formed cherry bomb or globe torpedo is produced. This method is most likely the way perfectly round globe salutes and torpedoes were made.

It is obvious firecracker companies were trying to sell their new version of the M-80 by association with the military; this implied military bomb, which in turn meant "big boom" in the minds of consumers. Because of this, the M-80 and larger firecrackers began to be compared in strength to dynamite, although these

comparisons were utterly ridiculous. Even the largest firecrackers did not come close to the explosive power of a stick of dynamite. This myth has been perpetuated to this day by pre–4th of July warnings by so many fire marshals blowing up watermelons all across America as a way of warning or scaring mostly young boys away from firecrackers. Flash powder is classified as a low explosive and burns at a much slower rate than nitroglycerin, the explosive ingredient in dynamite. While flash powder burns, creating pressure in a confined container to cause an explosion, dynamite (a high explosive) explodes by detonation. Detonation is the process whereby the material being detonated is consumed all at the same instant, creating supersonic shock waves, whereas flash powder sound waves are subsonic.

With the passage of time, the various sizes of American-made salutes and their respective standards of size and comparisons to dynamite have become more pronounced. The latter applies especially to illegal bootleg firecrackers. Since 1966, all firecrackers, salutes, or any other non-aerial exploding firework have been limited by federal law to contain no more than fifty milligrams of explosive powder. Makers of legally-made firecrackers sold since 1966 may try to cash in on the uninformed buyer who has heard tales of the good old days, with names such as M-80, M-100, Double M-80, M-1000, or M-10 billion—it doesn't matter what you call it, if it is a legal firecracker sold in the United States today, it contains less than fifty milligrams of powder. On the other hand, illegal firecrackers are still being made, bought, and sold in the US and are named in relation to the power of dynamite for marketing purposes. Today's underground firecrackers have names like "Super M-80," "M-1000," "M-250," "Quarter Stick," "Half Stick," and "Full Stick." All of these are fabricated names made to create an association with dynamite that simply does not exist. This obsession with the destructive explosive power of these firecrackers is what caused all the problems in the first place. Anyone making firecrackers of this type without a BATF (Bureau of Alcohol, Tobacco, Firearms, and Explosives) license faces becoming a felon with severe state and federal penalties, including fines and prison time. That is, if you don't blow yourself up first. America's firecracker past, along with present-day terrorist acts, have made the whole world wary and vigilant of any type of bomb maker or explosion—celebratory or not.

Chapter 4

Firecrackers and the American Industrial Revolution

In the beginning all large American firecrackers were made by hand. Later innovations made it much easier to make salutes. No longer was it necessary to have skilled workers produce firecrackers as it had been with the Chinese firecracker. The salute was simplified, and now almost anybody could put one together in short order. All it required in the way of materials was a paper tube casing, a charge of the new flash powder (of which there were now many different formulas), two end plugs, a little glue, and a fuse. This meant the factories could hire unskilled workers and have them producing up to speed in a relatively short period of time. All that was needed to increase production was to expand the factory and hire more workers. But all the while, as with all growing business endeavors, owners of the firecracker factories were looking for new methods and materials to improve production and profits.

By the 1900s, machines were helping make everything produced in America. Much money and success could come to the entrepreneur who could figure out how to do any given task with a machine. Where once the Chinese had to make firecrackers completely by hand using only the most primitive hand tools, new machines were being invented all the time to handle the most mundane and repetitive tasks. Tube rolling, fuse making, and powder mixing could all be done with various machines. One of the greatest time savers and major improvements to the firecracker was the invention of what is known as "visco" fuse and the machine that makes it. Visco fuse starts out like the Chinese firecracker fuse, with small grains of black powder wrapped in paper, but it does not stop there. It is then wrapped with

thread spirally in one direction, then the other direction, and is finally coated with a nitrocellulose lacquer that makes a super tough, highly reliable, waterproof fuse. No longer was the tedious yet highly skilled job of rolling fuse by hand required. This new visco fuse could be made in different diameters and packaged on spools of up to 5,000 feet, and could be easily cut into small pieces as needed by hand or machine directly from the spool. The tube-rolling machines also increased production a hundred times over from the slow and tedious job previously done by highly skilled individuals. The quality of the machine-made tubes was always consistent and perfect, whereas those rolled by hand produced a certain percentage that were inferior and could not be used. The machined tubes could be produced rapidly in any size needed. Workers were still needed to run the machines, and assembly, finishing, and packaging was still done by hand. Production was increased more than a hundredfold with these new machines, but demand was increasing just as fast. Factories were sprouting up like mushrooms across the country and the firecrackers just kept getting bigger and more diverse in style and shape. By 1950, the figures were most astonishing indeed: in 1950, the world's largest firework factory produced 100,000,000 salutes, along with 35,000,000 sparklers and 3,000,000 roman candles.

During this era of the Great American Firecracker, with such large profits to be made and the ease of manufacturing, hundreds of manufacturing companies sprung up practically overnight. Some of these disappeared as fast as they appeared, either being forced out of business by the competition, producing inferior products, or getting blown to smithereens. In researching this book, it was my goal to discover and recognize every American firecracker manufacturer from 1900 to 1966, but this has been an impossible task. Many of the smaller makers have disappeared without a trace and sufficient time has passed that virtually no records or products remain. Other companies produced firecrackers in such great variation and numbers that many of the highly collectible products, boxes, packaging, or business papers still exist. I have personally cataloged and valued over 175 boxes from various companies in this book (see chapter 6). Several of the larger American firecracker makers were munitions manufacturers during the war and switched to fireworks in peacetime, and many of the workers at munitions plants started their own companies after the war with the skills they learned. Some of the largest, most productive, and best known American companies were:

• Hitts Fireworks, Seattle, Washington
• Unexcelled Manufacturing Company, New York

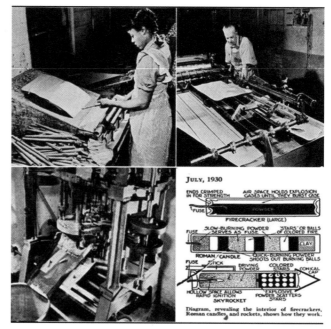

Clockwise from top left: 1. A girl rolls firework tubes with a simple hand-fed machine, doing the pasting as she goes circa 1930. 2. This machine does the same thing automatically circa 1950. 3. An automatic rotary plate machine feeds in firecracker tubes, crimps the bottom to seal, puts in about fifty grains of powder, fuses, crimps the top, and expels the finished product for packaging, mid-1950s. 4. Typical products of manufacture. *Popular Science Magazine*

• Arrow Fireworks Co., Inc., Cleveland, Ohio
• M. Backes & Sons, Wallingford, Connecticut
• Essex Specialty Co., Berkley Heights, New Jersey
• Edmund S. Hunt and Sons Co., Weymouth, Massachusetts
• New Jersey Fireworks Manufacturing Co., Vineland, New Jersey
• Gropper Brothers, New York, NY
• Havre De Grace Fireworks Co., Inc., Havre De Grace, Maryland
• Kent Manufacturing Company, Chestertown, Maryland
• L. W. Loyd Co., Inc., South Pittsburg, Tennessee
• Miller Fireworks & Novelty Co., Inc., Holland, Ohio
• National Fireworks Co., Elkton, Maryland

Most all of these companies had many branches in different parts of the country for manufacturing and distribution. Some of the larger companies made products that were sold by a company other than the manufacturer. This exchange also happened when it came to the packaging artwork, which was often shared. Boxes of cherry bombs that looked the same in every respect on the outside often had three different manufacturers' names on the package and three slightly different products on the inside. All of this competition led to many new innovations in the way firecrackers were produced. From 1900 to 1930, there was a rush for new ideas. Many new patents were issued for new ingenious devices and various types of explosive fireworks. Most of these new patents led to improved products, more productive manufacturing processes, and products that were safer to use. Most of the greatest advances in the American firecracker were the work of just one man, Thomas Gabriel Hitt. But before we take a look at his contributions, let us take a look at the odd, weird, and just plain silly items and inventions that were part of the great firecracker evolution in America.

Firecracker safety has always been a concern, probably ever since its invention. Most likely much of the concern arose out of fear of the loud noise and startling nature of the device, rather than actual harm or injury. After all, they do sound like weapons being discharged. Any person that has had a firecracker explode behind their back when they were not expecting it can attest to the instant anxiety, irritation, and fear they can cause. These concerns became greatly exaggerated by newspapers quoting unfounded statistics of children being killed, maimed, and blinded, or houses being burned down by the use of Chinese firecrackers. In 1952, a *Saturday Evening Post* editorial claimed that fireworks (in general) had "killed or wounded 11 times more Americans than the Revolutionary War." Every year after the 4th of July, newspapers would publish statistics about the number of injuries and deaths caused by celebrations, lots of times insinuating or confusing the facts by including drownings, automobile accidents, etc., along with firework injury statistics. There has always been an anti-firework lobby in America and probably always will be. The truth is, before the advent of the large American salutes and cannon crackers, the Chinese imports really weren't all that dangerous. Sure, they could split your fingers open and cause burns if not handled properly and sometimes a particle might get into your eye, and they were not the best things for children to play with without proper instruction, but there were lots of common everyday things that were just as dangerous or worse. As the Chinese firecracker was replaced by the American salute and sizes slowly climbed to twelve inches or better, so too did the risk of serious injury or death. It

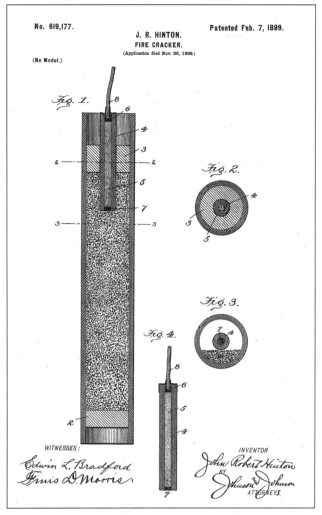

J. R. Hinton's patent of February 7, 1899, for a device he simply called Fire Cracker. This improvement to the way large cannon crackers were fused consisted of a tube containing a whistle composition that the fire had to pass through before reaching the explosive charge causing detonation.

was now possible to actually do what the naysayers had always claimed was already happening. Fingers could be blown off. You could be blinded, maimed, or even killed using these firecrackers. Manufacturers of salutes and cannon crackers paid attention to the outcry over safety issues and tried to quell protests by making their products safer, if not in practice then at least in appearance.

One attempt to make salutes and crackers safer to use resulted early on in a patent. In 1899, a man named J. R. Hinton observed that some fuses, especially on the large cannon crackers, could be unreliable. They could sputter and hiss and appear to go out, but all the while still held a glowing ember of fire that could reignite the fuse again at any time. This effect could be devastating to inexperienced firecracker users, whose first instinct was to assume the firecracker fuse had gone out and pick up the firecracker for examination, seeing if it could be relit or at the very least dissected to retrieve the explosive powder. This big mistake could easily end in serious disaster. But from the perspective of an invincible young boy that was a whole penny down the drain. Who in their right mind would waste such a valuable commodity as an unexploded firecracker? Of course, the proper thing to do was to leave the firecracker alone and wait an hour or even overnight, and then it could be safely retrieved. But who had the time or patience for that! This all too common situation caused many injuries and lost fingers, so J. R. Hinton came up with an ingenious solution: he devised a fuse for large cannon crackers that consisted of a regular fuse that first ignited a secondary fuse tube inside the cannon cracker. This inner tube was filled with a whistle composition. For the cannon cracker to detonate, it had to burn through about three seconds of a very loud whistling noise first. This meant if you lit the cannon cracker and it did not go off and you assumed the fuse had gone completely out but it was really still smoldering, you could safely approach and even pick up the cracker. If, upon doing so, you suddenly heard a loud whistling sound, you would know the cracker was about to go off and would immediately throw it down, thereby saving your fingers and perhaps your whole hand. This seemed like a great safety feature for the large cannon crackers, but it is unclear if any crackers of this type were ever marketed with emphasis on the safety aspects. Similar crackers were produced with the whistling characteristic emphasized with names such as Triumph's Screaming Bomb, Silver Streak, Sputtering Devils, and Musical Salutes.

The whistling fuse warning system described in J. R. Hinton's 1899 patent seems like a really good idea that would have contributed greatly to firecracker safety, but in a rush to improve the safety record of the large salutes that had always threatened the firecracker business, some pretty silly inventions would be patented. Just as Hinton's patent for the whistling fuse addressed a common firecracker problem, so too did the not-so-practical invention of Koby Kohn in 1924. Maybe you could call it bravado, maybe just the stupidity of youth or some other strange rite of passage, but if you got a group of boys together lighting large firecrackers, more

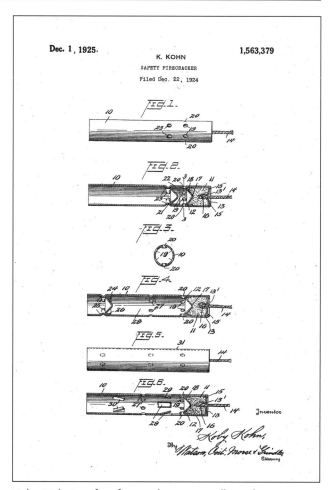

Koby Kohn's safety firecracker was really nothing more than a short firecracker placed in a much longer tube that acted as a handle to hold while lighting the firecracker. This was an impractical solution to the serious problem of children holding firecrackers in their hands while lighting. A better idea was to print "Do Not Hold in Hand" on the package and the 'crackers, although neither seemed to work.

often than not it would lead to a sort of pyrotechnic game of chicken. Chicken, as most people know, is a game of dare in which the participants see who is the most insane while risking serious injury by being the last to flinch. The game was made most popular in the 1950s, again by totally insane people—usually teenagers—driving their cars head on at full speed towards each other. The one that turned away first was labeled a chicken. This was a big problem with young boys way back when with the big firecrackers. The object of the game was to light and hold a salute in your hand longer than your opponent, throwing it at the last possible moment. Never mind such factors as both parties usually could not light their firecracker at exactly

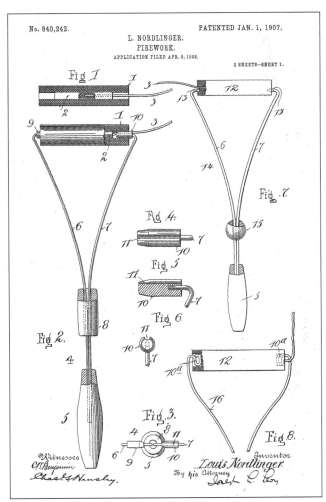

No. 840,242.   PATENTED JAN. 1, 1907.
L. NORDLINGER.
FIREWORK.
APPLICATION FILED APR. 9, 1906.
2 SHEETS—SHEET 1.

Nordlinger's patent for a silly firecracker and firecracker holder combination was probably invented to address the firecracker safety issue. This might have sold to worried mothers, but young boys would not be bothered with such nonsense.

the same time, or that fuses were of slightly different lengths and burned at slightly different rates, placing someone at a disadvantage from the start of the contest. Needless to say, this game often ended in real tragedy.

Along comes Koby Kohn (who would later patent some great designs for torpedoes) with a solution to the "chicken" problem. In December 1924, he filed for and received a patent for what he called the "safety firecracker." How's that for an oxymoron! Could there ever be such a thing? Well, Mr. Kohn came up with a firecracker of considerable power that could be safely held in the hand during detonation—well, sort of at least, depending on where you held it. In his 1924 patent application Mr. Kohn states:

It is well-known that the ordinary firecracker or salute, as it is sometimes known, is not considered safe, especially in the hands of children or irresponsible persons. This is mostly because of the danger of the firecracker exploding while still held in the hand. It is the usual practice to hold the firecracker by the end remote from the fuse with one hand lighting the fuse from a match or other source of fire held in the other hand, and it may be that the fuse acts quicker than expected, or that the users attention is distracted, and the firecracker explodes in his hand, resulting in painful injuries if not the loss of several fingers. The present invention contemplates overcoming these difficulties by providing the safety firecracker in which the charges confined near the end containing the fuse and by providing a weakened section in the side walls just behind the explosive charge containing section.

In other words, despite all the fancy drawings and explanations, this was a firecracker with a long tube in which the explosive was placed at one end with a weakened wall right behind the charge and an empty tube acting as a handle. In theory, when it exploded it would break off and leave the shooter holding half of the empty tube. There were a few flaws behind this, foremost being the fact that users of fireworks were told ad nauseam "Do Not Hold in Hand" and now suddenly it was OK to hold one in your hand. That kind of mixed signal could be confusing to a young boy. And if you could safely hold a powerful firecracker in your hand while it went off, where would you hold it? Well, right in front of your face, of course, where you could see it going off. What if you did not hold it at the very end? What if you had large hands that extended into the danger zone? What if the "weakened walls" turned out to be not so weak? I doubt if Mr. Kohn's "safety firecracker" ever saw the light of day.

Perhaps the strangest patent related to firecrackers and safety was invented by Louis Nordlinger of New York, who was granted a patent for his unnamed device on New Years day in 1907. It was a downright weird contraption for safely holding and exploding a firecracker. Mr. Nordlinger was certainly playing off the worries of America's mothers when he came up with this device. The patent contains three different versions of the device. The main version required the purchase of special firecrackers made especially for this device. These firecrackers had no end caps. Without end caps or plugs a firecracker cannot build up enough pressure to explode. Instead, the powder just burns, throwing sparks out the ends until the fuel is spent. In order for these special firecrackers to explode they had to be clamped between the arms of this device. On the ends of these arms were the necessary end caps that would allow the firecracker to explode, so the end caps would be clamped over the ends of the cap-less cracker, the fuse was passed through a slot in the cap, and then the whole device could be held by the wooden handle while the fuse was lit. The firecracker could then explode, sending the caps outward, and you were ready to start the whole process again. Oh what fun this must have been. Can't you just see all the worried mothers putting their sons through all that just to light a firecracker? And the device was probably every bit as dangerous as the firecracker itself, especially since, in what must have been a moment of doubt on Mr. Norlinger's part

as to where people would buy both the special firecrackers and the special holder, he also submitted two additional designs for his device that could be used with any type of firecracker. I am sure many of these devices ended up in the trash heap after somebody tried to light a mighty twelve-incher, if they were even sold at all.

A lot of thought, time, and money went into how to make the firecracker safer. At the same time, a lot of thought was going into how to make them bigger, faster, cheaper, and more attractive to the main consumer, young boys. While it was great to ease mothers' fears of little Johnny blowing a few of his fingers off, at the same time little Johnny did not want his firecrackers labeled "safe." Boys wanted big and loud. They wanted to throw them up in the air, shoot them out of slingshots, put them under cans, blow up watermelons, and scare girls. This was the tightrope the firework manufacturers were trying to walk, and ever so slowly they were losing their balance.

Chapter 5

Thomas G. Hitt: America's Firecracker Genius

Thomas Gabriel Hitt was born in London in 1874, and began his long and distinguished firework career in 1898. Shortly thereafter, he and his brother started the Hitt Fireworks Company in Victoria, British Columbia. In 1905, he relocated the company to the Columbia City district of Seattle, Washington. T. G. Hitt established one of the safest and most successful fireworks companies in the United States. He was a fireworks genius, an innovator who held many patents on firework production and presentation. T. G. Hitt and his associates at the Hitt Fireworks Company did more for the advancement of firecrackers in America than any other group. With the invention of photographic flash powder and the publication of *The Art of Fireworks* circa 1898 came a whole new wave of possibilities for the firework industry. Riding the crest of that wave was the Hitt Company, particularly a bright young pyrotechnician named William E. Priestly. After some experimentation with "flash" compositions they came up with a new powder formula for the Chinese firecracker. They called the new crackers "flashlight" firecrackers and immediately set off to China to find a manufacturer for the American "flash cracker." The new "flashlight crackers," made from the addition of magnesium powder to the traditional black powder, created a brilliant flash of white light when they exploded and added a new spark to the commonplace Chinese firecracker that Hitt knew the American consumer would love. By this time flash powder formulations had become fairly widespread in America, but Hitt was the first to introduce it to the Chinese. He found resistance to the new powder by the traditional family makers of firecrackers that he

had used in the past. They were used to centuries-old traditions and materials for making their firecrackers and were not so eager to change. Priestly decided

Hitt's first "flashlight" firecracker was named Navy Brand and was made in China. It was a product of the new factory set up by William E. Priestly, another pyrotechnic wizard.

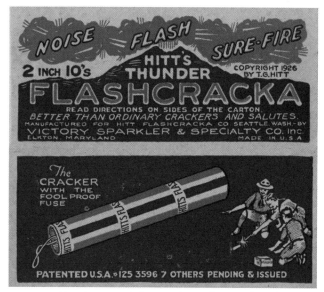

Front and back artwork from a box of Hitt's Thunder Flashcrackas, America's first best-selling two-inch salute circa 1926. Hitt used both "Sure Fire" and "Foolproof Fuse" are used to emphasize the safety of the product.

he would open his own factory in China to make the new flash crackers for the American market. Priestly set up his new factory in Hong Kong and began making the new "Navy Brand" "Hitt's Chinese Flashcracka's," adding the new variation to the word flash cracker to the label that would later become a Hitt trademark. The term flash cracker was new but could not be copyrighted, but the new word "flashcracka" could be copyrighted. Hitt was hoping that by adding the new word to his new product people would associate any flash-powder-based firecracker yet to come as being exclusively his company's product and people would ask for them by name.

As it turned out, the Chinese were right about working with the new sensitive flash powder and the new factory promptly blew up, killing thirty employees. Undeterred, Priestly set up a new factory on an island in the Pearl River and began again, this time employing new safety ideas he had learned from the previous disaster. Some, such as the use of many small, lightly constructed "blow away buildings" instead of one central production building made of heavy materials, and using separate buildings for each operation involved in making the cracker, would be adopted as standard safety practice by all companies to follow.

T. G. Hitt was a true innovator in the art and business of fireworks. Building upon the success of his Chinese-made flashlight crackers, Hitt took the next step in America, making a new line of two-inch cannon crackers. Hitt's Thunder Flashcrackas would become the best-selling American salute of all time. Compared to the lowly Chinese firecracker it had a huge explosion and brilliant flash of light. The "Flashcracka" was advertised heavily as "the best firecracker obtainable anywhere, at any time or at any price," and Americans seemed to agree.

Lighting firecrackers was not as straightforward as it seems. Those that would become experienced lighting firecrackers learned what to look for, but novices often learned the hard way with burns or injuries. There were lots of quirks and things to look out for that could go wrong. It was very important to understand the nature of the beast and the only way to do that was through experience or a good teacher. Firecrackers did not come with a user manual. A firecracker that did not explode became known as a "dud." Out of any quantity of firecrackers there were always a certain percentage of duds. There were many reasons this might happen.

HITT'S FLASHCRACKAS

Genuine Hitt's Flash Crackas, an old standby and the original flash salute. Loud reports and bright flashes.

2-in. box of 5 pieces 5c;   6 for 25c
3-in. box of 4 pieces 5c;   6 for 25c
5-in. box of 2 pieces 5c;   6 for 25c
Case of 100 packages_ _ _ _ _ _ _ _ _$4.00

Mail order catalog ad for various sizes of genuine Hitt's "Flashcrackas." Millions of Hitt's salutes were sold via mail to the hungry American public, making the firecrackers available to many who would otherwise not have access to them.

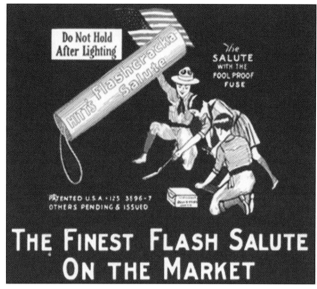

THE FINEST FLASH SALUTE ON THE MARKET

Hitt's "flashcracka" advertisement sent subtle messages to the firecracker consumer. In addition to the safety factor of the fuse, young American scouts waving the flag conveyed patriotism and the addition of a girl to the picture suggested firecrackers weren't just for boys. Also notice the firecracker is lighted on the ground—not in a hand—and the boys have an ample quantity of salutes to light. Hitt tried to cover all the concerns of the American consumer.

Sometimes the fuse could have a void where the powder was not in a continuous line, making it go out. Sometimes the fuse got pulled slightly out of the explosive powder so the fuse was consumed before ever reaching the charge. For whatever reason, duds were an aggravation to the consumer and dangerous to young boys who could not stand to see a good firecracker go to waste. They might be tempted to try to light a ⅛-inch fuse stub sticking out of an unexploded firecracker or pick up what appeared to be a dud but was actually still smoldering—both situations that could end in disaster. Another factor was lighting the fuse. The firecracker fuse was designed to burn at a designated rate, giving the user an ample "burn time" of about five seconds to either get away or throw it (as was usually the case). But one was only given this much time if the fuse was lit properly at the very end; it was possible to light the fuse in the middle or any place other than the very end, thus unexpectedly reducing the "burn time" one could hold on to the cracker before it exploded. If one was not totally aware of the immediate situation of having your five seconds reduced to two seconds, again possible disaster. This happened more often than one might expect, especially in the frenzy of a group of young boys all lighting firecrackers together, lighting them at night, or one boy holding the cracker while another lit it. In an attempt to convince worried mothers and others concerned about injuries caused by salutes, Hitt very cleverly addressed the "dud" problem with the introduction of a new fuse. The term "Fool Proof Fuse" would seem to infer it was not possible to light the firecracker incorrectly, making it safer. Hitt's "Fool

Proof Fuse" was simply a long fuse doubled over into a loop, thereby entering the explosive charge in two places instead of one and doubling the chances the firecracker would go off. Increasing the live-to-dud ratio by 50% helped with children picking up duds, but because it could be lit anywhere along its length, it was not really fool proof. Here is what Hitt had to say about his "Fool Proof Fuse" in his patent application:

…the fuse being so positioned in connection with the explosive material 4 that the looped portion 12 is located at a suitable distance beyond one end of the tapered tubular section 1, thereby forming a fuse having a considerably higher degree of efficiency than the fuse at present commonly used in the manufacture of 'fire crackers. In lighting or setting the looped 'end of the fuse as described in this application, it is obvious, that two lighted end portions will find their way into the explosive matter or it may be that one of the ends will become extinguished while the other end will perform the required duty.

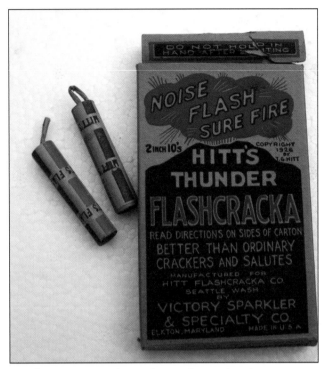

Another variation of Hitt's best selling "Thunder Flashcrackas" with a couple examples of the double-fused crackers. Early on Hitt's Co., which was located on the west coast, teamed up with Victory Fireworks on the east coast to cover the whole country and cut down on shipping costs.

Another variation of Hitt's popular two-inch "Thunder Flashcracka." This is a small five-piece box that was made to add into large fireworks display assortment boxes made for family 4th of July celebrations. Made under contract with the Victory Sparkler & Specialty Company, Inc. of Elkton, Maryland.

With the huge success of the two-inch Flashcracka and the ever-increasing public demand for a bigger bang, the Hitt factory started to make bigger cannon crackers and packaging them in various quantities to cover all levels of the American market. Soon demand for the quality of the Hitt brand was more than the Hitt factory could produce. To meet this demand Hitt began subcontracting other companies to make their products with the Hitt brand on them. He found that having a manufacturer/distributor on the east coast meant shipping costs could be greatly reduced. His choice for production on the east coast would be an established fireworks company that produced mostly sparklers, the Victory Sparkler Company of Elkton, Maryland, in an area of the country that would eventually become dotted with firework companies and be known as the fireworks highway. Hitt firecrackers were the first of the Great American Firecrackers.

And the hits just kept on coming! Somewhere along the line in their experiments with flash powder, the pyrotechnicians at the Hitt factory made a discovery that seemed almost impossible at the time: he invented the plug-less firecracker. Up until this time it was assumed that to cause the necessary explosion, a composition had to be contained in a sealed container of considerable strength, depending on the sensitivity of said composition. The faster a composition burned the weaker the containment could be. Hitt filed for a patent for his new "plug less" firecracker on August 2, 1917, and his new formula for improved flash powder on August 27, 1917, and received both patents on January 15, 1918. According to information in his patent, the main reason for the new "plug less" firecracker design was:

> to lessen the danger to children and inexperienced persons who fire them. It has been the common practice to close the ends of firecrackers with clay that dries hard; with wooden plugs, and other materials that are driven away in solid form by the explosion, rendering crackers to some extent dangerous. The object of this invention is to entirely dispense with the plugs.

Hitt no doubt realized he could also streamline production in this way and eliminate some of the most labor intensive steps involved in the manufacture of firecrackers, improving production output by simply

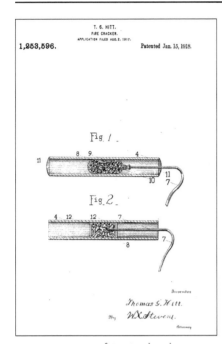

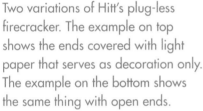

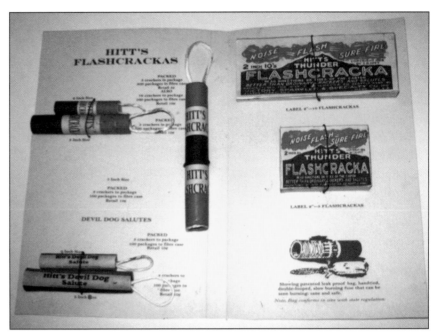

Two variations of Hitt's plug-less firecracker. The example on top shows the ends covered with light paper that serves as decoration only. The example on the bottom shows the same thing with open ends.

A very rare Hitt's Flashcracka salesman's sample display. In addition to several different sizes of firecracka, Hitt also began peddling his "Devil Dog" brand. These Devil Dog firecrackers were virtually the same as the flashcracka at this stage, but would take many different forms over the years.

doing away with the end plugs. His constant experimenting with new powder formulas and the mechanics of the workings of the firecracker earned him a dozen or so patents over the years. Experience had taught him that ordinary firecrackers containing black powder would need to be tightly contained to cause the necessary pressure to build up after ignition for an explosion. Therefore, it made sense that the more sensitive the powder was, the less complex the "container" would have to be to produce the desired detonation and explosion. If a powder composition could be produced that would explode inside just a couple layers of paper and all that was needed was a means of transferring fire (fuse) to a quantity of powder, virtually anything could become a firecracker.

Hitt also realized the dangerous nature of photo flash compositions commonly in use at the time that were made with chlorate of potash (potassium chlorate). His first firecracker patent dealing with the explosive chemical composition replaced potassium chlorate with a much safer chemical, potassium perchlorate. This new powder variation was almost as sensitive to detonation but was much safer to mix and handle. In his original United States patent office application Hitt writes:

Heretofore, the powder used in firecrackers has usually been made of chlorate of potassium mixed with various organic substances, but such compounds using chlorate as a base, are dangerous in mixing, dangerous from percussion, dangerous in handling, and liable to spontaneous combustion in storage. Therefore, the object of this invention is to produce a firecracker that shall be entirely safe under the conditions above stated, and yet possesses equal or greater detonating power. To make the powder, I take of the following ingredients, first pulverized:

Perchlorate of potassium.................. 16 parts

Aluminum.. 14 parts

Sulphur... 5 parts

Mix them thoroughly. Then secure in the cracker body a charge of this powder proportionate to the loudness of detonation desired. If the charge was as large as that of other powders commonly used, this cracker will produce a very much louder detonation than others, and, when fired in the dark it will give a broader and more brilliant flare. Perchlorate of potassium combined with the ingredients stated, or their equivalents, in about the proportions described, has never to my knowledge been exploded in mixing or by percussion, or by spontaneous combustion yet. With all of these advantages for safety, there is no material difference in the cost of manufacture.

This seemingly simple substitution of chemicals was probably the single greatest contribution to firecracker manufacturing safety. The combination of potassium chlorate and sulphur has always been known as an extremely sensitive and unpredictable combination prone to spontaneous combustion by any number of causes previously mentioned in Hitt's patent. Almost every firework factory accident had this combination of chemicals as the singular cause. George Wiengart warned in his book on making fireworks that even the accidental scraping of a fingernail on a mixing sieve was enough to cause the potassium chlorate mixture to explode. Up until the time of Hitt's new flash powder patent, all flash powders had been made with potassium chlorate. Today US law prohibits the use of potassium chlorate in firework compounds entirely, except for miniscule amounts in a few very small novelty items.

It was the invention of this new and powerful flash formula that made it possible to create the plug-less firecracker. The powder is enclosed in a bag of thin, strong paper. The fuse enters the mouth of the bag that is wrapped and tied with a string, preventing the fuse being pulled out. The bag is placed in the middle of an ordinary cardboard tube. The ends are not plugged or capped. The detonation of the powder occurs so fast and fierce that, due to atmospheric pressure, the air inside the tube cannot be displaced fast enough, creating "plugs of air" at the ends of the tube and causing an explosion to occur.

Thomas G. Hitt's second American firecracker patent seems very odd and out of place. It is unknown if any of the following items were actually produced and sold, but it is doubtful, and no examples are known to exist.

On February 12, 1918, T. G. Hitt was awarded a patent for a device he simply called a "burglar alarm." This device was three of his large firecrackers with the fuses tied together. The theory behind this weird invention

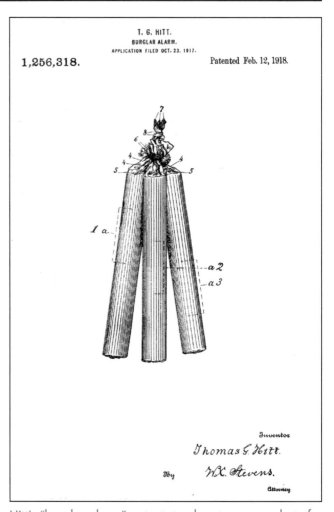

T. G. HITT.
BURGLAR ALARM.
APPLICATION FILED OCT. 23, 1917.

1,256,318.

Patented Feb. 12, 1918.

Inventor
Thomas G. Hitt.
By
W.X. Stevens.
Attorney

Hitt's "burglar alarm" patent stands out as somewhat of a "dud" in comparison to his other brilliant discoveries. Not as elaborate as a Rube Goldberg invention, but very much reminiscent.

is best described by Hitt himself. Again quoting from his patent application, he writes:

> This invention relates to burglar alarms, and its object is to provide means whereby persons in their own residences, or traveling by carriage, automobile, railway car or other conveyance may give the signal of distress, for example: like three quick reports of a revolver, accompanied each by a bright flashlight to disclose their locality in case of attempted burglary, highway robbery, house on fire or other sudden danger demanding the aid of neighbors or the police.

It seems that most burglaries occur when the occupant of the house is not at home. Perhaps when you left your house for any extended period of time you were supposed

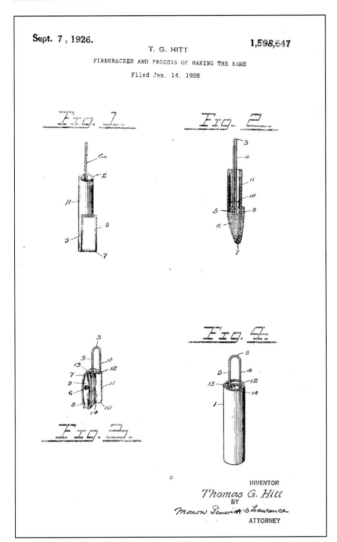

Sept. 7, 1926.

T. G. HITT

FIRECRACKER AND PROCESS OF MAKING THE SAME

1,598,647

Filed Jan. 14, 1926

Fig. 1.   *Fig. 2.*

Fig. 3.   *Fig. 4.*

INVENTOR
Thomas G. Hitt
BY
Mason Fenwick & Lawrence
ATTORNEY

T. G. Hitt's September 7, 1926, "Firecracker and process of Making the Same" patent had very little new to offer, other than a newly designed "Sure Fire" fuse. This patent was mostly how to solve the problem of locating the explosive bag in the center of the tube. Here the problem is solved by creating spring tension with the folded paper bag, applying glue, and pushing down to the halfway point.

to leave this device in plain sight on the table with a note reading "Dear Burglar, On the table you will find a bundle of 3 firecrackers and a box of matches. Could you please light these and throw them out the window before stealing all of my worldly possessions? Thank you." With all of the millions of firecrackers and firearms in the possession of Americans at any given time in 1926, one has to wonder if the inventor actually believed anyone would pay attention to three firecrackers going off and say to themselves, "Oh, somebody must be in distress, I had better summon help!" Hitt's description

suggests why this might not have been the greatest idea. He relates the device's operation to simulating three revolver shots and a bright flashlight. I would wager a guess that any burglar breaking and entering an occupied home or business would be much more discouraged by revolver shots and a bright flashlight than three firecrackers. Maybe it is just the great difference in the times we live in versus the days gone by that makes this invention seem so ridiculous. Hitt does state in his patent that the proper authorities would need to familiarize themselves with the sound of this device to be able to recognize it as a distress signal, which does not lend any practicality to the device.

Actually, the only thing that made this item patentable was the timing effect. Each firecracker's explosive charge was placed in a different part of a tube: the first firecracker had the charge at the top of the tube, the second in the middle, and the third at the bottom, with the fuses all running to a bundle that was tied together at the top. Once the device was lighted, the firecrackers would explode in timed succession because the fuses were actually of different lengths relative to the placement of the explosive charges, thereby adjusting the detonation timing automatically. Thus, the burglar alarm patent was awarded more as a timing invention rather than a firecracker innovation.

Hitt's next three firecracker patents were all basically improvements to his first firecracker patent, adding just minor changes in design or manufacturing procedure, and were granted in 1926 and 1927. There is not much of interest in these patents for the firecracker enthusiast, as they were merely attempts to solve problems or improve upon his previous work.

One of the problems Hitt ran into with his first firecracker patent was fitting the powder bag precisely in the center of the firecracker tube. Since the bags were handmade and filled separately from the tube and then both were assembled, sometimes the powder bag was a little too small and slid right through and sometimes it was a little too big and required some stuffing to get it in place, all contributing to a lot of lost production time. He tried to remedy the problem with his next two patents. He must have worked on this problem for some time, because it was not suitably solved until his patent of 1931. Both patents of 1926 were related to how to fold the bag containing the powder so as to put pressure on the inner walls to hold the bag in the center of the tube with sealing wax. The 1927 patent dealt with basically the same problem solved in the same manner as the previous patent, with the most noticeable difference being the tube. The tube was of narrowing diameter as it went from top to bottom, with the wider flare at the top. This allowed the explosive bag to be easily inserted in the flared tube end while increasing frictional resistance from the ever-narrowing walls until the powder bag would be firmly attached inside the interior box-like container already built into the main firecracker tube. An ingenious design, but still not quite right for what he had in mind for ease of construction.

Both of these patents featured improvements to the "Fool Proof Fuse." It was now securely held in place by folds in the powder bag and could not be pulled out. It also now ran the entire length along both sides of the explosive charge. It was advertised that it was like having two fuses on every "Flashcracka" and the words "Sure Fire" in big bold letters were added to the boxes. Again, it reduced the dud problem even more.

Finally, on August 23, 1932, Hitt solved all of the problems with firecracker design that had begun fourteen years previous. With patent number 1,873,202, titled "Manufacturer of Firecrackers," he solved all of the issues of all the previous designs in a brilliant stroke of simplicity. In his patent, Hitt laid out the problems he had in the past very precisely. He wrote:

> The prime object is to construct a fire cracker consisting of a bag filled with an explosive placed in a tube intermediate the ends of said, the ends of the tube being open in such a manner that there will be no chance for wrinkles or twisted bags which sometimes occurs when the bags are filled independent of the tube and afterwards forced therein. Heretofore the tubes have been rolled in a certain length and diameter, and the bags formed independent of the tube and filled with the explosive, the fuse placed in the bag and the same tied, after which the bag is forced into the tube. As these bags are handmade and filled, it is almost impossible to have a uniform bag that exactly fits the tube. Invariably the bag is either slightly undersized or oversize. Where the bag is undersized, an inferior detonation results as the gases have a chance to escape from the confining bag into the air- space between the tube and the bag before the detonation occurs. In the case of the

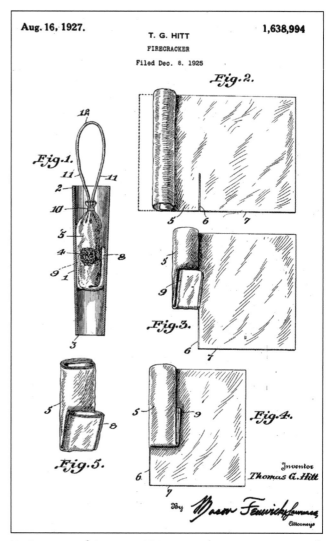

Hitt's patent of August 1927. In another attempt to speed up the production of 'crackers and solve the problem of the powder bag being mounted in the very center of the casing, Hitt devised a way to make the outer casing slightly narrower at the bottom (Fig. 1). This constriction in the casing was designed to stop the powder bag at the halfway point.

> oversize bag, the same becomes twisted or bent in being forced into the tube which may result in a burning instead of a detonation, or a plurality of weak explosions.

This is very telling of Hitt's obsession to build the perfect firecracker. Not a grain of powder was to be wasted by not detonating and each firecracker had to perform as good as the last one. A great deal of observation of previous products had led him to a simple solution and a point closer to firecracker perfection. He describes the solution to the problem thusly:

By placing the empty bag in the tube on a former and then filling the same with the explosive after the former has been removed, a uniform tight fit is always obtained which results in a loud detonation and a very superior structure, with the bag containing the explosive charge being always closely adjacent the inner wall of the tube.

Hitt also addressed a minor problem of powder leakage around where the fuse was inserted. The process was now so simple it could be done by machine and not only by hand. Simply stated, it worked like this: the firecracker tube was placed on a nipple that stopped the bag former at the right position (Fig. 1). A light strong paper was placed over a wooden dowel (former) the same size as the diameter of the tube. The paper and former were pushed into the tube, leaving enough paper sticking out of the top to facilitate tying the bag and fuse (Fig. 2). The bag was then filled with a measured amount of explosive powder and a fuse and the bag was sealed and tied shut (Fig. 3). A small amount of adhesive was dabbed into the tube from the bottom to hold the explosive bag in place. Then the explosive bag was pushed down into the center of the tube and, voila, the perfect cannon cracker had been constructed.

Hitt and his business partner Wilfred Priestly also held several other patents related to firecrackers, mostly involving the way firecrackers were strung together, packaged, etc. These patents are probably of little interest to the reader and are outside the scope of this book.

At some point Hitt turned the emphasis on his firecrackers from the loudness of the report to the brilliant flash of light and colors that could be produced as a byproduct of the explosion. He knew that the tube containing the firecracker could somewhat diminish the flash of the explosion, so he set out to make a firecracker whose:

principal object is to provide a structure which will produce the maximum flash with the detonation, but particularly for the production of colored flash detonations, since the short outer tube does not interfere with the depth and brilliancy of the color.

This new firecracker had a radical new design and looked like his old firecracker turned inside out. The bag containing the powder charge was now twice the size of the firecracker tube it was in and protruded from both ends of the firecracker tube. Hitt writes:

With the advent of flash compositions, it has become highly desirable to have a flash as well as the detonation. As a result of numerous tests and experiments, I have found that by extending the tube beyond the explosive interior, detonation is obtained but that the extension of the tube serves to smother the flash. By having the bag containing the flash and explosive composition extend slightly beyond the tube, a much superior flash is obtained, and at the same time, the walls of the tube confine the explosive sufficiently to result in the detonation.

This was no doubt the first firecracker to be developed specifically to produce the most brilliant flash possible and with the addition of color. Once again, Hitt also redesigned the fusing for this firecracker, with maybe a touch of overkill, or perhaps he had some trouble or complaints about ignition problems. Whatever the reason, this new cracker had no less than four fuses running most of the way through the explosive composition. It must have been impossible to have a dud with these. Hitt does not mention the type of falsh powder used or what additives and colors the flashes were with this cracker. It must have been spectacular to watch one of these go off. Hitt called his new firecracker "Devil Dogs." Hitt describes his new flash bomb and compares it to his past works in his patent application:

The principal object is to provide a structure which will produce the maximum flash with a detonation, but particularly for the production of colored flash detonations, since the short outer tube does not interfere with the depth and brilliancy of the color.

In my invention covered by Letters Patent No. 1,253,596, I stated that it was not necessary to use a plug, wad, or other means for closing the end of the tube, as by having a substantial length of tube project beyond the explosive, a cushion of air was formed which acted in exactly

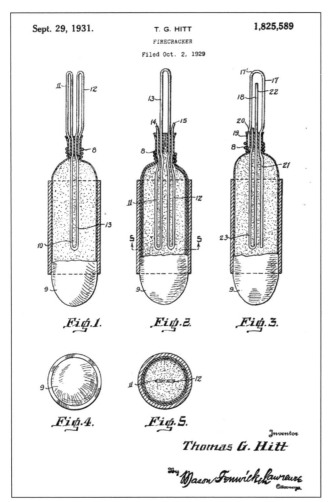

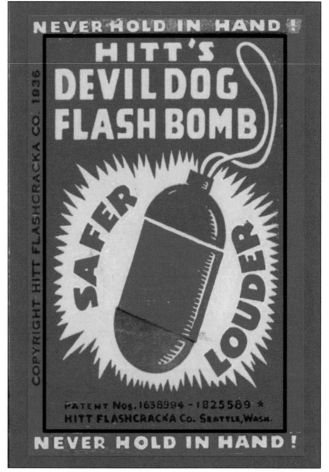

With the "Devi Dog" patent Hitt went for more flash than bang by turning his previous designs inside out to put the accent on the flash instead of the bang. He also used chemicals to make colored flashes and improved the fuse by making no less than four fuses to ignite the composition.

A new version of Hitt's Devil Dog salute. This replaced the old Devil Dog, which was basically the same as the flashcracka, with a new larger firecracker that produced the most brilliant flash yet and in color.

the same manner as the so plug to confine the gases and result in an explosion when the same was ignited.

With the advent of flash compositions, as covered in my Letters Patent No. 1,253,597, it became highly desirable to have a flash as well as detonation. As a result of numerous tests and experiments, I have found that by extending the tube beyond the explosive, superior detonation is obtained, but that the extension of the tube serves to also smother the flash. By having the bag containing the flash and explosive composition extend slightly beyond the tube, a much superior flash is obtained, and at the same time, the walls of the tube confine the

explosive sufficiently to result in a detonation.

When I remove the tube altogether from the bag; where the bag has a very thin wrapping, no detonation results, there being merely a flash. But, where the tube surrounded the bag, I found a very substantial detonation was obtained, although not as superior as where the tube extended beyond the end of the explosive.

The Hitt company was the only firework manufacturer on record to concentrate any research on the beautiful side of explosive fireworks. This may have been market related, because sales and the use of salutes were almost exclusively male driven, or it was possibly an attempt to make a "pretty" salute that would appeal to women and girls. T. G. Hitt was very successful in the business of fireworks, but he was also a pyrotechnics artist, visionary, and genius. After all, the salute and firecracker

Rare early 1900s photograph of one of Hitt's displays showing aerial pyrotechnics effects that are no longer produced today. Hitt was a true innovator in all that he did in pyrotechnics.

Although famous for quality firecrackers, Hitt's main business was his famous display work. Here is a letter dated November 3, 1926, congratulating Hitt and Co. for the extraordinary quality of twenty-four displays put on for the country's 150-year birthday.

T. G. Hitt and his wife (c. 1920) preparing an enormous aerial display shell for launch. This was most likely to be a test of a new design or effect.

were merely a small part of the Hitt operation. The Hitt Fireworks Company was much more famous worldwide for their beautiful, innovative displays that were the heart of the business. Perhaps his artistry took over from the mundane business of the manufacture of explosive fireworks in later years. Indeed, his last two patents for explosive fireworks concentrated on the brilliant beauty that could be found in the heart of an explosion. The invention of the Devil Dog salute, concentrating on the brilliance of the flash and adding color, would lead him to his grandest firecracker of all.

In the world of art there is the term "masterwork" or "masterpiece" that refers to the most outstanding piece of work in a respective artistic format—the pinnacle of artistic accomplishment. Thomas G. Hitt was certainly a creative and innovative artist, and fire was his medium. As previously noted, he was world renowned for his spectacular displays and reenactments, like his nearly full-scale "Burning of Atlanta" reenactment. But when one is speaking strictly about firecrackers with nothing else in consideration, it is hard for one to see just how anything remotely artistic could ever be accomplished. While most of the effort in making firecrackers in the last century concentrated on making

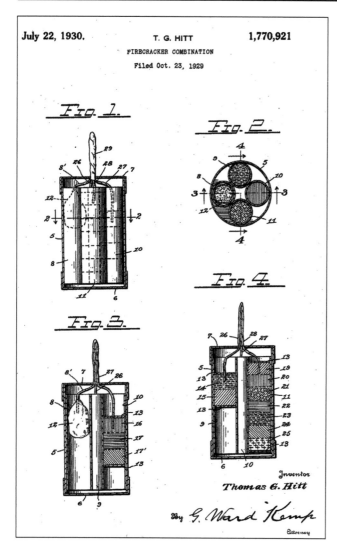

July 22, 1930.　　　T. G. HITT　　　1,770,921

FIRECRACKER COMBINATION

Filed Oct. 23, 1929

Fig. 1.

Fig. 2.

Fig. 3.

Fig. 4.

Inventor
Thomas G. Hitt
By *G. Ward Kemp*
Attorney

Hitt invented the most complicated and beautiful firecracker ever! A color-changing series of thirteen detonations, each more spectacular than the other. For collectors, this is the Holy Grail. It is unclear if this device ever went into production and no existing specimen has ever been found.

One of the last known images of the Hitt offices located in a section of Seattle, Washington, and affectionately know as Hitt's Hill, c. 1960.

a bigger boom and making it faster, cheaper, and sometimes safer, to most, a firecracker is something you lay on the ground, light the fuse, it goes off with varying degrees of Ka-boom! and flash, and then it is repeated. Pretty boring. Which is why boys and young men (forever the biggest consumer of crackers and salutes) would always come up with new and novel ways to use them. Unless you are young, the firecracker is just another noisemaker in a world filled with noise. Hitt broke the firecracker mold with his experiments in brilliance and color, two qualities of Hitt's display work that surpassed any competition and undoubtedly had a lot to do with his invention of the most spectacular firecracker ever

invented. Hitt's masterwork firecracker, patent number 1770921, is shrouded in mystery. Most serious collectors today are unaware of its existence. It is not known if this device was ever put into production or not and no known examples have been found, but any firecracker aficionado who saw one go off would never forget it. For any serious firecracker collector to find an original, unspent Hitt's patent number 1770921 would be like finding the Holy Grail.

Hitt's patent, granted October 23, 1929, was simply called "Firecracker Combination," which is an understatement. In appearance, it looked like the world's biggest firecracker on the outside (which in itself is saying a lot in the days of twelve-inch and larger firecrackers). Hitt described it as a "giant imitation firecracker." The single large tube contained an elaborate and complicated construction on the inside. The complexity of this device may well be the reason it was never produced in any quantity. On the inside, four different tubes, all designed to perform a different effect at a different time, were arranged and time fused to perform a ballet of explosions and brilliant flashes of light and color. So what made it so special?

Instead of quoting from Hitt's often dry and technical patent applications, let me rather describe the incredible performance artistry from the viewpoint of a firecracker enthusiast. Allow me to imagine that from the moment you set the firecracker on the ground, you have no idea what to expect from the biggest firecracker you have ever seen. Lighting the fuse and stepping back a safe distance, you get exactly what you might expect. First to go off is a large and powerful eight-inch flashcracker.

It goes off with a tremendous, earth shaking, teeth rattling KA-BOOM, accompanied by a large flash of brilliant white light that definitely gets your attention. You do not see it in the dark, but the first explosion has broken the main container into bits, exposing the rest of the workings. Then there are two more simultaneous large explosions, this time with a brilliant red flash and a brilliant green flash. Next are a series of three consecutive large explosions one right behind the other with brilliant red, white, and blue colored flashes. And then comes the finale of seven simultaneous explosions, all with brilliant colored flashes of all the colors of the rainbow (red, orange, yellow, green, blue, indigo, and violet) all in a row. That had to be the ultimate firecracker.

Chapter 6

Great American Firecracker Collectibles Identification and Value Guide

From early in the twentieth century until about 1960, American firecracker companies were fiercely competitive for their share of the market. With literally hundreds of brands and types being manufactured and sold, the manufacturers used various means to target their consumer base. The greatest emphasis on marketing became brand loyalty. The products and the market were constantly changing. With some exceptions (such as Hitt's Flashcrackas, which seemed to sell well every year), new types of firecrackers would only last a few years on the market, but if you could convince the consumer that your brand was superior to others, brand loyalty could be established and customers would seek out a company's newest offering, as well as old standbys. Since all firecrackers might seem the same to the inexperienced or first-time user, packaging and artwork became important selling tools. Learning from the Chinese firecracker makers, manufacturers came up with eye-catching designs to attract attention to their products. Certain color schemes (usually patriotic red, white, and blue) and patriotic imagery, such as Lady Liberty, Uncle Sam, flags, bunting, and the Liberty Bell, were common. So were images of large explosions, even atomic bomb explosions. This suggested one company's firecracker was much more powerful than the competition's. As accidents began to increase and safety became an issue, companies would feature cartoon drawings or pictures of children playing with firecrackers to make them look more harmless. All of this marketing and packaging did sell firecrackers, but when it came right down to it, all a boy wanted was the most explosive power he could buy for the least amount of money.

Most boys worked for months, saving their nickels in anticipation of 4th of July purchases. Knowing this, a lot of manufacturers spared the expense of the fancy packaging and put up their goods in plain white boxes that simply said "Salutes" or "M-80s" on the front of the box. The typical twelve-year-old would usually give great consideration to his 4th of July purchases. Author Bradford Smith, reminiscing about his 1920 4th of July experience in his book *Pilgram Boy*, gives some insight into what it must have been like for a young boy of eleven. He writes:

> Early in June we had begun to make our plans, because fireworks cost money and money had to be earned. There was a great deal of lawn-mowing and errand running, and the movies had to get along without our eleven cents admission fees. Then, a few days ahead, paper signs saying "Fireworks" were pasted to the sides of temporary shacks. As we lined up to buy, most of us had lists to follow. We wanted the largest possible amount of noise for our money, so as a rule we invested heavily in the biggest salutes the law would allow. Then we bought Chinese firecrackers, ranging in size from two or 3 inches to little inch long ones which we usually set off a whole package at a time.
>
> Women were not expected to have any part of it, except perhaps when mothers were called to bind up burned hands.

Because we are human, we reminisce. Wonderful memories! All those wonderful 4th of Julys and the firecrackers of our youth are now a thing of the past, which is why we want them back again. Firecrackers and the boxes they came in are highly collectible today. As with any paper packaging, almost all of it was discarded and thrown away, which is why it is so rare and collectible today. I began picking up and collecting discarded cannon cracker, cherry bomb, torpedo, and salute boxes when I was about seven or eight years old. My friends all liked the colorful Chinese firecracker labels much better, so I would grab all of these I could to be used as barter material.

Over the years I have added to my collection, with the goal of acquiring or at least documenting every single large American-made salute, cannon cracker, cherry bomb, or torpedo box ever made. Now I realize this to be an impossible goal, as some are just gone forever. This book is the accumulation of more than forty years of collecting American salutes, boxes, and

materials, yet I am still often presented with a salute or box I have not seen before.

Collecting American firecrackers can be an exciting and rewarding hobby and has become very popular, especially online. Auction sites and collector forums often offer salute boxes for sale. A few websites like CuriosityEmporium.com even sell reproductions of the old boxes, posters, signs, and catalogs, although these are clearly marked as reproductions. The novice collector needs to be wary of originals versus reproductions. Here are some of the things to watch for when collecting these items.

First of all, there is a huge dilemma for the collector to deal with: "live" versus "neutralized" firecrackers. Live firecrackers are those that contain all of the explosive powder and are unaltered in any way since they were manufactured. They are also illegal to possess in all fifty states. "Neutralized" firecrackers are just what they sound like: vintage firecrackers that have had their explosive materials removed or rendered harmless by emptying the powder, injecting resins, or by some other method. If done correctly, this maintains the look of the firecracker while still making it inert, legal, and safe to ship. Therein lies the dilemma. Despite all the reasons not to, most serious collectors of American firecrackers only collect live firecrackers and look upon neutralization as the destruction of historical items, even though the appearance is fully preserved and the absence of the explosive charge cannot be detected unless the firecracker is lit, which they never plan to do in the first place. While all of this may seem highly illogical from the layperson's point of view, every day vintage "live" firecrackers are bought and sold.

The difference in the value of live firecrackers compared to neutralized ones can be immense. For example, one of the rarest of all salutes is a box of ten "Buck Rogers Disintegrators" made by the National Fireworks Company in 1936. A box in mint condition with all ten pieces that had been neutralized recently brought $640 on one auction website. A few weeks later, a somewhat ragged box with only eight of the ten live salutes was being offered for $3,400. With price discrepancies this great and such a large demand, it is no wonder that a vast underground market exists, and a not-so-underground market as well. The biggest auction of vintage firecrackers ever held had to be that of George Moyer's outstanding world-class collection of more than forty years. It was held on June 22 and 23, 2012, simultaneously at Morphy's auction house in Pennsylvania and on the internet. This single auction grossed over $450,000 and most all of the items sold were live, vintage American firecrackers. This auction included some of the biggest and most powerful American firecrackers ever made. The auction was so successful that a second, smaller auction was held on July 26, 2015, but the results of that auction were not available at the time of this writing.

So for the new collector, I would say only collect neutralized firecrackers, or just the boxes they came in, though most long-time collectors will disagree with me on this point. I believe it is possible to have a wonderful collection and preserve this special time in America's history by limiting your collection to non-explosive items that meet today's legal and safety concerns. Most collectors who have live salutes in their collection never intend to set them off anyway, so what difference should it make?

Here are some guidelines for your collection:

1. As already discussed, a box with some content is worth more than just an empty box. For display purposes, it is nice to have at least one example of what was in the box and what it looked like. I see no reason why this can't be a non-functioning piece, but collectors will use their own discretion.

2. Condition is everything. Values depend on two major things: the rarity of the item and the condition it is in. Like any other paper-product collectible, the boxes salutes came in were mostly disposed of, and that is what creates rarity. It is still possible to find rare boxes in unused condition. Every so often discoveries are made of unused packaging and even gold-mine finds of whole, unopened cases of goods.

3. Check internet auctions and join collectors' forums to find items for sale or trade. Firecracker and salute collectors are passionate about their hobby just like any other collector, and will be happy to talk to you about collecting.

4. Never pass up an opportunity to buy more than one of an item if the price is right. You can always use the duplicates to barter for something else you do not have for your collection. Bartering is half the fun!

5. Watch out for reproductions. Just like any other collecting hobby, reproductions are out there. While it is OK to add reproductions to your collection—especially reproductions of really rare items you will probably never find or maybe can't afford—avoid reproductions that are represented as original items. Most legitimate makers of reproductions clearly mark their items as reproductions somewhere on the item itself. Collecting American salute boxes is an investment, so rare original boxes will appreciate in value, but reproductions may not.

6. If you purchase live vintage firecrackers and would like to have them neutralized for your collection, do not attempt this yourself. Seek the advice of a licensed pyrotechnition or somebody with experience dealing with live firecrackers.

7. Think about the children. If you absolutely insist on collecting live salutes, store them in a place where children have absolutely no chance of getting to them. Remember, you are taking a chance. Do not put the firecrackers behind glass or near sources of

open flame or electricity.

8. A really good place to start pyrobilia collecting is vintage catalogs. Mail order was a big part of firecracker marketing. Collecting catalogs is a good way to see what all was available and when. Some of the catalogs were very elaborate and contained full-color pictures and attractive original artwork.

What follows are pictures and approximate values of some of the Great American Firecrackers. This is probably the most comprehensive value guide relating to the subject of Great American Firecrackers yet to be created, but it is far from complete. Some specimens have vanished forever with the passage of time.

A word about values and prices: the price of pyrobilia is determined by many factors—just like any other collectible—among them rarity, condition, and demand. With American firecrackers, value is also determined by the contents of the box. Is the box full and sealed, opened and partially full, or is it just an empty box? With American firecrackers, prices have always been on the rise, which makes them a great investment, as witnessed at the Morphy's auction. These results came as a pleasant surprise to long-time collectors everywhere and set a new standard for values. Since then, many of these auction items have been sold and resold and the prices have continued to rise. With so many variables, it is difficult to put a set value on individual items. Like anything else, value is often determined solely upon how much someone will pay for it. The following price guide was compiled using online auctions and other online sales, along with the help of many collectors who

buy and sell on a regular basis, and is both current and comprehensive at this time. Because of the many variables, I have displayed the values of the individual items with a range from low to high. This covers most of the items you are likely to come across. The lower of these values would be a box, without content, in very good to mint condition, meaning no major damage to the box itself: no stains, rips, creases, folds, or water damage. Boxes in lesser condition would be valued less proportionately with the damage to the box. The top number expresses a box in mint to very good condition with most of its original contents included. The quantity of original salutes included also affects the value of an item, with lesser quantities being valued proportionately lower and full boxes valued higher. Unopened boxes in mint condition are exceedingly rare and highly sought after. Accordingly, an unopened box in mint condition is the most desirable and would be worth considerably more than the highest value listed here.

All of the listings in this chapter are loosely arranged by manufacturer and are presented with the following information and format:

Name of Item, date of manufacture, Company name and address, number of pieces, value of a single box only in good to mint condition – value of full box of original contents in good to mint condition.

American Torpedoes, c. 1920s, American Fireworks Company, 6 pieces, rare $60–$300.

Generic Flash Salutes, c. 1930, Unknown Manufacturer, Elkton, Maryland, 8 pieces, $25–$100.

Atomic Bulldog Salutes, c. 1940, L. W. Loyd Co., Inc., South Pittsburg, Tennessee, 144 pieces, $100–$350.

Super Silver Salutes, c.1940–1960, American Fireworks Co., Mehoopany, Pennsylvania, 72 pieces, common $25–$100.

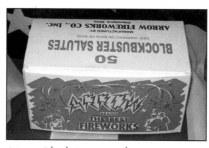

Arrow Block Buster Salutes, c. 1940, Arrow Firework Co. Inc., Cleveland, Ohio, 50 pieces, $30–$180.

Cub Scout Salutes, c. 1935, Essex Specialty Co., Elkton, Maryland, 8 pieces, rare $100–$300.

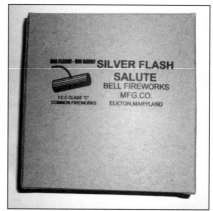

Silver Flash Salute, c. 1950s, Bell Fireworks Mfg. Co., Elkton, Maryland, 72 pieces, $25–$150.

Big Bang Salutes, c. 1940s, M. Backes' & Sons, Wallingford, Connecticut, 50 pieces, $40–$225.

Big Bang Flash Salutes, c. 1940s, Manufacturer Unknown, 12 pieces, $90–$200.

Pyramid Flash Salutes, c. 1930, Dixie Fireworks Mfg. Co., Piedmont, Alabama, number of pieces unknown, very rare $200–$600.

Essex Brand, c. 1940, Essex Specialty Co., Inc., Berkeley Heights, New Jersey, 12 pieces, $40–$240.

Celebrated Silver Electric Torpedoes, c. 1920, Gropper Brothers, New York, 12 pieces, $100–$350.

Halco Radio Salutes, c. 1945, Halco, made in USA, 6 pieces, $65–$250.

Buck Rogers Disintegrators, 1936, The National Fireworks Company, Elkton, Maryland, 10 pieces. One of the rarest boxes, this item came boxed with a toy cannon named "The Battle for Mars" that shot the lighted salutes out. $250–$2000.

Gee Whiz, The All American Bang, c. 1948, American Fireworks Co., Mehoopany, Pennsylvania, 5 pieces, rare, $60–$180.

Doughboy Salutes, Halco, c. 1940 (although these were made in China, they were made for the US market and were popular here), 72 pieces, $75–$400.

Uncle Sam Gold Flash, c. 1900, Edmund S. Hunt & Sons Co., Weymouth, Massachusetts, 12 pieces, $50–$400.

Silver Flash Salutes, c. 1930, Essex Specialty Co., Inc., Berkeley Heights, New Jersey, 12 pieces, $50–$300.

Globe Flash Salutes, c. 1920, Victory Fireworks & Specialty Co., Elkton, Maryland, 72 pieces, $75–$300.

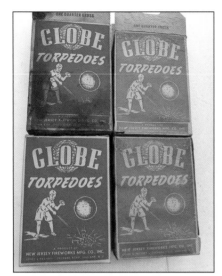

Globe Torpedoes, c. 1930, New Jersey Fireworks Mfg., Co., Inc., Vineland New Jersey, 36 pieces, $80–$350.

Havre De Grace Cherry Torpedoes, c. 1920, Havre De Grace Fireworks Co., Inc., Havre De Grace, Maryland, 36 pieces, rare $150–$500.

Halco Midget Flash Salutes, c. 1940, Halco, made in China for US market, 20 pieces, rare, $100–$300.

Hitt's Thunder Flashcracka, c. 1940, Victory Sparkler & Specialty Co., Inc., Elkton Maryland, 10 pieces, rarer version of Flaschcracka box, $65–$350.

Kent Cherry Flash Salutes, c. 1940–1960, Kent Manufacturing Corporation, Chestertown, Maryland, 5 pieces, Common $40–$150.

Kent Cherry Flash Salutes, c. 1940–1960, Kent Manufacturing Corporation, Chestertown, Maryland, 72 pieces, Common $50–$500.

Kent Brand 2 inch Salutes, c. 1930, Kent Manufacturing Corporation, Chestertown, Maryland, 50 pieces, $75–$600.

Hitt's Devil Dog Flash Bomb, 1936, Hitt Flashcracka Co., Inc., Seattle, Washington, number of pieces unknown, rare $150–$900.

Hitts Thunder Flashcracka (box only), c. 1920, Victory Sparkler & Specialty Co., Inc., Elkton Maryland, 10 pieces. There were many different styles and sizes of the Hitt's Flashcracka box. Thousands of this particular box were rescued from the factory in Elkton, Maryland, and as a result, it is very common, with a value of around $10.

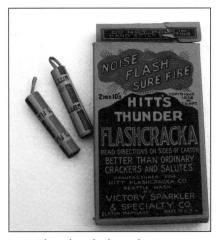

Hitt's Thunder Flashcracka, c. 1920–1940, Victory Sparkler & Specialty Co., Inc., Elkton Maryland, 10 pieces—vertical version of the box above—$25–$200.

Bearcat Torpedoes, c. 1920, M. Backes' Sons, Inc., Wallingford, Connecticut, 10 pieces, rare $100–$300.

Keystone Super Silver Salutes, c. 1950, Keystone Fireworks Co., Inc., Elkton, Maryland, 72 pieces, $40–$250.

Kent Kannon Krackers, c. 1940–1950, Kent Manufacturing Corporation, Chestertown, Maryland, 144 pieces, $75–$1000.

Miller Silver Salutes, c. 1940, Miller Fireworks & Novelty Co., Inc., Holland, Ohio, 72 pieces, $75–$500.

Bearcat Torpedoes, c. 1930, M. Backes' Sons, Inc., Wallingford, Connecticut, 72 pieces, rare $150–$800.

Hitt's Devil Dog Salutes, c. 1930, Hitt Firework Company, Columbia City, Washington, 72 pieces, rare $100–$600.

Miller Cherry Bombs, c. 1940, Miller Fireworks & Novelty Co., Inc., Holland, Ohio, 72 pieces, $75–$500.

Miller Silver Salutes, c. 1960, Miller Fireworks & Novelty Co., Inc., Holland, Ohio, 72 pieces, $40–$400.

Miller M-80 Firecrackers, c. 1960, Miller Fireworks & Novelty Co., Inc., 301 Glengary Road, Holland, Ohio, Common 72 pieces, $40–$500.

Miller Silver Salute, c. 1960, Miller Fireworks & Novelty Co., Inc., Holland, Ohio, 72 pieces, $75–$500.

Miller Silver Tube Salutes, c. 1940, Miller Fireworks & Novelty Co., Inc., 301 Glengary Road, Holland, Ohio, common 72 pieces, $75–$500.

Miller M-80 Firecrackers, c. 1960, Miller Fireworks & Novelty Co., Dekalb, Missouri, 36 pieces, packed in paper bags $10–$200.

National M-80 Salutes, c. 1930, National Fireworks Co., Inc., Elkton, Maryland, 144 pieces, very rare $250–$1000.

National Salutes 2 Inch, c. 1930, National Fireworks Co., Inc., Elkton, Maryland, 12 pieces, rare $75– $200.

National Salutes 2 Inch, c. 1930, National Fireworks Co., Inc., Elkton, Maryland, 12 pieces, rare $75– $300.

National Bantam Torpedoes, c. 1930, National Fireworks Co., Inc., Elkton, Maryland, 12 pieces, rare $75–$300.

National Bantam Torpedoes, c. 1920, National Fireworks Co., Inc., Elkton, Maryland, 72 pieces, rare $100–$600.

National Salutes 2 Inch, c. 1940, National Fireworks Co., Inc., Elkton, Maryland, 50 pieces, rare $75– $300

National Electric Dragon Flash Salutes, National Fireworks Co., Inc., Elkton, Maryland, Top: 2 inches, c. 1920, 10 pieces, $75– $300. Middle: 2 inch, c. 1920, 5 pieces, $50–$200. Bottom: 3 inches, c. 1920, 5 pieces, $75–$300.

National Electric Dragon 5 inch, c. 1920, National Fireworks Co., Inc., Elkton, Maryland, 50 pieces, very rare $200–$1000+.

New Jersey Fireworks Cherry Flash Salutes, New Jersey Fireworks Mfg. Co., Inc., Vineland, New Jersey, and Elkton, Maryland, c. 1930, $75–$500.

New Jersey Fireworks Cherry Flash Salutes, c. 1920, New Jersey Fireworks Mfg. Co., Inc., Vineland, New Jersey, and Elkton, Maryland, 72 pieces, $100–$800.

National Square Shooters, c. 1930, National Fireworks Co., Inc., Elkton, Maryland, 12 pieces, rare $75–$350.

New Jersey Fireworks Cherry Flash Salutes, New Jersey Fireworks Mfg. Co., Inc., Vineland, New Jersey, and Elkton, Maryland, c. 1930, 10 gross packed 20½ gross boxes (1,440 pieces), exceedingly rare, unopened case value unknown.

New Jersey Fireworks Big Bang Salutes, New Jersey Fireworks Mfg. Co., Inc., Vineland, New Jersey and Elkton, Maryland, c. 1930, 12 pieces, very rare $150–$600.

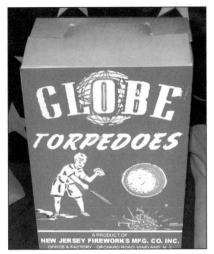

Globe Torpedoes, New Jersey Fireworks Mfg. Co., Inc., Vineland, New Jersey, and Elkton, Maryland, c. 1930, 72 pieces, $75–$600.

Little Giant Safety Torpedoes, New Jersey Fireworks Mfg. Co., Inc., Vineland, New Jersey, and Elkton, Maryland, c. 1930, 12 pieces, rare $100–$600.

New Jersey Fireworks Super Bull Dog Salutes, c. 1945, New Jersey Fireworks Mfg. Co., Inc., Vineland, New Jersey, and Elkton, Maryland, 72 pieces, $75–$200.

Atomic Flash Bang M-80 Salutes, c. 1940, Nordlinger-Charlton Fireworks Co., Inc., 72 pieces, very rare, $200–$800.

New Jersey Fireworks Pest Control Bombs, c. 1960, New Jersey Fireworks Mfg. Co., Inc., Vineland, New Jersey, and Elkton, Maryland, 144 pieces each box. Note: after the Child Protection Act of 1966 was signed outlawing large firecrackers, companies were allowed ten years (5 years in text) to phase out their old stockpiles. Many companies continued to sell their products to the agriculture industry in the guise of pest control devices to scare off birds. In some cases the manufacturers used old stock boxes and simply pasted a new label over existing boxes. These "paste overs" are worth slightly more than the actual pest control boxes. Common $40–$300.

Ozark Crackers, c. 1960, Maker Unknown, 72 pieces, common $15–$150.

Silver Streak Super Sonic Whistle Salutes, c. 1945, manufacturer unknown, 12 pieces, rare $50–$400.

Spitfire Spray Salutes, c. 1950, Apollo of the Ozarks, PO Box 25, Stanton, Missouri, 144 pieces, $45–$350.

Star Brand Liberty Torpedo, c. 1915, M. Backes' Sons, Inc., Wallingford, Connecticut, 12 pieces, rare $75–$600.

Big Bang Flash Salutes, c. 1939, Essex Specialty Co. Inc., Berkeley Heights, New Jersey, 12 pieces, $50–$300.

Sputtering Devil Salutes, c. 1910, Manufacturer Unknown, 12 pieces, extremely rare $100–$650.

Star Brand Salutes, c. 1920, M. Backes' Sons, Inc., Wallingford, Connecticut, 100 pieces, rare $150–$1000.

Star Brand Salutes 2 inch, c. 1920, M. Backes' Sons, Inc., Wallingford, Connecticut, 50 pieces, rare $40–$800.

Noi-Zee Boy Tube Flash Salute, c. 1932, The Spencer Fireworks Co., Polk, Ohio, 144 pieces, rare $75–$500.

Standard Cherry Bombs, c. 1950, Standard Fireworks and Manufacturing Co. Inc., Elkton, Maryland, 24 pieces, $25–$200.

Star Brand Salutes, c. 1920, M. Backes' Sons, Inc., Wallingford, Connecticut, 8 pieces, rare $60–$250.

Star Brand Salutes, c. 1930, M. Backes' Sons, Inc., Wallingford, Connecticut, 10 pieces, $45–$350.

Star Brand Glittacracks, c. 1930, M. Backes' Sons, Inc., Wallingford, Connecticut, 10 pieces, rare $75–$900.

Star Brand Sailor Salutes 2 inch, c. 1920, M. Backes' Sons, Inc., Wallingford, Connecticut, 10 pieces, rare $75–$350.

Star Brand Electric Silver Torpedoes, c. 1915, M. Backes' Sons, Inc., Wallingford, Connecticut, 6 pieces, rare $50–$750.

Lightning Flash Salute 8 inch, c. 1920, M. Backes' Sons, Inc., Wallingford, Connecticut, 2 pieces, rare $150–$1000.

Sunblast Flash Salute 5 inch, c. 1920, M. Backes' Sons, Inc., Wallingford, Connecticut, 1 piece, rare $100–$650.

T.N.T. Bombs Flash Salutes, c. 1950, Carolina Fireworks Mfg. Co., Clover, South Carolina, 72 pieces, $35–$250.

Star Brand Salutes, c. 1940, M. Backes' Sons, Inc., Wallingford, Connecticut, 10 pieces, $40–$250.

Star Brand Salutes Flash Salutes, c. 1920, M. Backes' Sons, Inc., Wallingford, Connecticut, 10 pieces, rare $150–$1000.

Texas Buster 2 Inch Salutes, c. 1945, Atlas Enterprises, Fort Worth, Texas, 50 pieces, $40–$300.

Star Brand Uncle Sam Salutes 2 Inch, c. 1920, M. Backes' Sons, Inc., Wallingford, Connecticut, 10 pieces, $50–$400.

Keystone M-80 Salutes, c. 1940, Keystone Fireworks Mfg. Co., Inc., Dunbar, Pennsylvainia, 72 pieces, $60–$350.

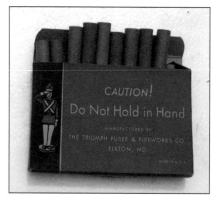

Triumph Toy Solider Salutes, c. 1929, The Triumph Fusee & Fireworks Co., Elkton, Maryland, 10 pieces, $40–$250.

Triumph Toy Solider Salutes, c. 1930, The Triumph Fusee & Fireworks Co., Elkton, Maryland, 10 pieces, $40–$250.

Triumph Cherry Bomb Flash Salutes, c. 1948, Spencer Novelty and Fireworks Co., Polk, Ohio, 72 pieces, $100–$650.

Triumph Colored Marble Salutes, c. 1935, The Triumph Fusee & Fireworks Co., Elkton, Maryland, 10 pieces, $40–$250.

Triumph Impact Flash Salutes, c. 1932, The Triumph Fusee & Fireworks Co., Elkton, Maryland, 36 pieces, rare $60–$350.

Triumph Screaming Bomb, c. 1929, The Triumph Fusee & Fireworks Co., Elkton, Maryland, 10 pieces, $75–$300.

Bomber 2 Inch Salutes, c. 1918, The Unexcelled Manufacturing Company, Inc., New York, NY, 50 pieces, $35–$200.

Buster 2 Inch Salutes, c. 1915, The Unexcelled Manufacturing Company, Inc., New York, NY, 10 pieces, $40–$150.

Boomer 3 Inch Salutes, c. 1920, The Unexcelled Manufacturing Company, Inc., New York, NY, 10 pieces, $40–$200.

UnXld (Green) 3 Inch Salutes, c. 1915, The Unexcelled Manufacturing Company, Inc., New York, NY, 6 pieces, $20–$150.

UnXld 5 Inch Salutes (Black Label), c. 1920, The Unexcelled Manufacturing Company, Inc., New York, NY, 8 pieces, $40–$250.

Big Noise 5 Inch Salutes, c. 1918, The Unexcelled Manufacturing Company, Inc., New York, NY, 8 pieces, $40–$350.

Big Noise 5 Inch Salutes, c. 1925, The Unexcelled Manufacturing Company, Inc., New York, NY, 24 pieces, $100–$400.

Challenge 2 Inch Salutes, c. 1918, The Unexcelled Manufacturing Company, Inc., New York, NY, 50 pieces, $100–$450.

Dandy 2 Inch Salutes, c. 1918, The Unexcelled Manufacturing Company, Inc., New York, NY, 100 pieces, $50–$650.

Boomer 3 Inch Salutes, c. 1915, The
Unexcelled Manufacturing Company,
Inc., New York, NY, 50 pieces,
$80–$450.

Lion 2 Inch Salutes, c. 1900, The
Unexcelled Manufacturing Company,
Inc., New York, NY, 16 pieces,
$60–$450.

Flash Limits 2 Inch Salutes, c. 1930,
The Unexcelled Manufacturing
Company, Inc., New York, NY, 10
pieces, $60–$250.

OK Salutes, c. 1930, The Unexcelled
Manufacturing Company, Inc., New
York, NY, 12 pieces, $40–$350.

Limits 2 Inch Salutes, c. 1930, The
Unexcelled Manufacturing Company,
Inc., New York, NY, 8 pieces,
$40–$250.

Big Noise 5 Inch Salutes, c. 1918,
The Unexcelled Manufacturing
Company, Inc., New York, NY, 5
pieces, $60–$450.

3 Packs of UnXld 2 Inch Green Label Salutes, c. 1920,
The Unexcelled Manufacturing Company, Inc., New
York, NY, Top two are 6 pieces each, bottom 8 pieces,
$60–$400.

Two Inch Salutes, c. 1945, United
Fireworks Mfg. Company Inc.,
Dayton, Ohio, 50 pieces, $25–
$250.

Victory 5 Inch Salutes, c. 1930, Victory Fireworks and Specialty Company, Elkton, Maryland, 12 pieces, $25–$250.

Musical Salutes, c. 1930, United Fireworks Mfg. Company Inc., Dayton, Ohio, 10 pieces, rare $60–$400.

Victory Step On Torpedoes, c. 1915, Victory Fireworks and Specialty Company, Elkton, Maryland, 36 pieces, rare $60–$500.

United (Cherry) Salutes, c. 1930–1950, United Fireworks Mfg. Company, Inc., Dayton, Ohio, 5 pieces, $25–$150.

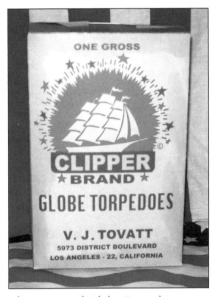

Clipper Brand Globe Torpedoes, date unknown, V. J. Tovatt, 5973 District Boulevard, Los Angeles, California, 144 pieces. rare box due to the fact California was not a fireworks manufacturing state, $150–$800.

Super Flash Blaster Salutes, c. 1950, StoneBraker Fireworks Mfg., Denver, Colorado, 72 pieces, very rare $100–$600.

Victory Cherry Bomb Salutes, c. 1940, Victory Fireworks and Specialty Company, 6 pieces, $40–$250.

Victory Globe Flash Salutes, c. 1920, Victory Fireworks and Specialty Company, 24 pieces, $40–$350.

Victory Safety Toy Torpedoes, c. 1945, Victory Sparkler and Specialty Company, Elkton, Maryland, 36 pieces, $25–$250.

Space Age Silver Salutes, c. 1950, StoneBraker Fireworks Mfg., Denver, Colorado, 72 pieces, very rare $100–$600.

Wooden M-80 military packing crate, c. 1968, Manufacturer unknown, quantity unknown, $100–$150.

Chapter 7

Factory Disasters: The Biggest Bangs of All

After WWII, America was anxious to get back to normal. Jobs were plentiful, and it was a time when women began to join the workforce previously dominated by men. Just about every fireworks manufacturer in America blew up at least once, sometimes two or three times. Most times these were small explosions that, while very scary, destroyed mostly property and not people, and were looked on as a mere occupational hazard. Everyone knew being a fireworks worker was a very dangerous occupation, but it paid well by the standards of the day (the average pay back then was thirty-eight cents an hour). The firework factories never had any trouble finding workers; indeed, people would move from several states away to get a good paying job in the fireworks industry. The town of Elkton, Maryland, saw its population grow from 3,500 to over 12,000 after adding employees at the Triumph Explosives plant. Most factories worked twenty-four-hour shifts, so there was lots of overtime available. Working sixty hours a week was not unheard of, and some employees would even work an occasional straight twenty-four-hour shift.

Incredible as it seems, the workers actually got used to smaller explosions as just part of the job. Before the big one in 1954 at the Kent factory there had been a lot of precursors in and around Elkton, Maryland: in June 1935, an explosion killed two workers; in October 1937, one man died in an explosion at the plant; on April 11, 1942, four women were seriously injured in an explosion and fire; on September 5, 1942, one person was killed and three were seriously injured in an explosion; on February 20, 1943, it was reported one man had died and three were seriously injured in an

M. Backes' Sons, Inc. fireworks factory as it appeared on the cover of one of its firework catalogs c. 1930. For safety reasons, factories consisted of many separate buildings and departments.

explosion; on May 8, 1943, a front page headline proclaimed "FIFTEEN KILLED: MANY INJURED BY EXPLOSION – FIRE"; and a September 4, 1944, *Whig* newspaper reported one young man killed in an explosion; and." Talk about occupational hazards! If you could get used to this, you could get used to just about anything.

Fireworks Alley: A Memoir

When WWII started in 1939, most of the big firework factories were converted to make munitions for the United States military. While fireworks were still being produced, they were now being made in greatly reduced quantities. The raw materials required to make fireworks were needed to make weapons of war and America was now struggling with shortages and rationing, and no longer had the extra money for such frivolities. The few Americans who could still afford to buy firecrackers for special occasions kept the existing producers in business until the war was over in 1945. As our victorious soldiers returned home, they brought with them a great need for celebration. America had been in a dark and miserable place for six long years. The American people had suffered at home and many had died on foreign shores. It was now time to celebrate the freedom that America's greatest generation had won and brought back home.

After the war, it was not an immediate return to normal for America's fireworks makers. Perhaps the last thing a shell shocked soldier wanted to hear was the Ka-boom of a cherry bomb or the machine gun fire of a firecracker string, or perhaps it took all those munitions plants a little time to convert to peacetime pursuits, but all that was soon to change. With the great war finally over, the country was now in the happiest of moods. It was a time of fantastic growth and prosperity. America turned its shortages into surplus, and families grew as the fastest population increase in America's history produced millions of "baby boomers." Was it just a coincidence they came up with the name "baby boomers?" Because if any generation loved the firecracker, it was the baby boomers! Housing developments sprung up overnight and for the first time in what seemed like an eternity, Americans enjoyed a much more relaxed lifestyle and disposable income. The postwar celebrations turned into holiday celebrations of barbecues, beach parties, and of course, fireworks!

Without munitions to make, the bullet and bomb factories soon turned their chemical expertise to

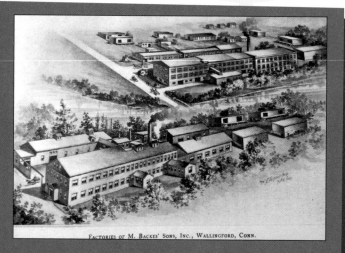

FACTORIES OF M. BACKES' SONS, INC., WALLINGFORD, CONN.

making fireworks and firecrackers. Once again business was booming, and so were the profits to be made, if you didn't mind the risks. In addition to converting munitions factories, many new factories were springing up as word of easy money spread. The biggest new factories were all located pretty close to each other in a few hot spots around the country, most notably Maryland, Ohio, and New Jersey. Smaller factories dotted the landscape from Georgia up through Tennessee to Missouri and the Ozark mountains. Out west you had Hitt's and others. The greatest concentration of firework factories in the country had to be along a stretch of road named Old Philadelphia Highway or State Road 7, known as Fireworks Alley. Most of these factories were in or near the town of Elkton, Maryland. The biggest names in fireworks manufacture all had a facility on Fireworks Alley at one time or another.

They say that once you smell black powder it gets in your blood and you are hooked for life. This was certainly true for Tony Fabrizi and Ken Lupoli, and all the other colorful characters along Fireworks Alley.

What's better than a kid in a candy store? A kid in a firecracker factory, that's what! And if that's the case, Ken Lupoli was probably one of the luckiest kids ever. Although Ken was born on the outside limits of the baby boomer years, his father, Pete Lupoli, was very much a part of the post-WWII firework industry through his associations. After the end of WWII, Pete Lupoli became friends with most

M. Backes' Sons, Inc. fireworks factory as it ended after years of explosions, relocations, and regulations severely limiting the production of fireworks. The rest was due to the ravages of time, as the owners finally admitted defeat and closed the doors forever, circa 1962.

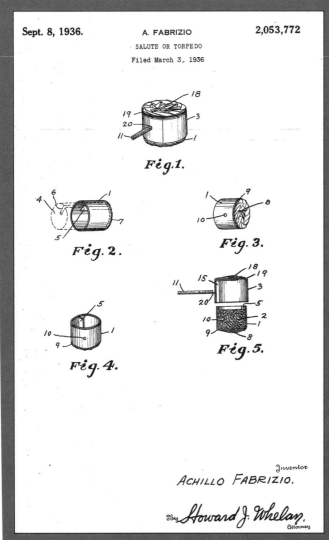

Sept. 8, 1936.   A. FABRIZIO   2,053,772

SALUTE OR TORPEDO

Filed March 3, 1936

Fig.1.

Fig.2.   *Fig.3.*

Fig.4.   *Fig.5.*

Inventor

ACHILLO FABRIZIO.

By *Howard J. Whelan.*
Attorney

Patent belonging to Achillo Fabrizio, whose son was one of the last of the great firecracker men along famous Fireworks Alley. This patent shows yet another design for a hockey-puck-shaped salute.

of the factory owners along Fireworks Alley. Pete was great friends with Tony Fabrizi, a fireworks legend of sorts. Tony was the owner of New Jersey Fireworks Co. (a.k.a. Kent Fireworks Co.), which at one time was one of the biggest producers of firecrackers in the US. Tony was once a worker for the Kent Firework Company and had survived the great explosion of 1954 (more on this soon). Despite this, he bought the place five years later and changed the name to New Jersey Fireworks Co. Somewhere along the line Tony had dropped the "o" from his name, changing from Fabrizio to Fabrizi. Tony was

the son of Achillo Fabrizio, who held several firework patents, including this one from 1936 for a unique salute design.

From the age of five, Ken Lupoli spent many weekends tagging along with his father, visiting his firework buddies along Fireworks Alley in Elkton, Maryland. He got to see the workings of the firecracker industry up close and personal and he never went home empty handed; Tony always made sure Ken had a couple boxes of this and a couple boxes of that to take home with him. He can recount fireworks tales from when he was five years old with such vivid detail you would think you were there. With almost all of the old timers now dead and gone, it becomes important for younger people who still have memories of the golden era of the Great American Firecracker to pass on their knowledge, lest it forever vanish into the annals of time.

Over the years, Pete and Ken Lupoli would become friends with most of the owners of the fireworks manufacturers along Fireworks Alley, who together produced most of the country's firecrackers in those waning years. There was Keystone Fireworks, owned by Joe Van Dyke, a pig farmer who also just happened to own a fireworks factory. Ken relates, "I remember very vividly, when you went to visit Joe Van Dyke at Keystone Fireworks, you first had to walk through rows of pig pens to get to the factory out back. It was a small operation that consisted of seven or eight small buildings." Joe also had another branch in Dunbar, Pennsylvania, and made Silver Salutes, as well as other small display items. Ken recalls that although everything made at Joe's was assembled by hand, they did have a tube rolling machine. "You could go there and watch them roll and cut tubes and make all the firecrackers. As a kid it was pretty impressive," Ken said.

When Tony Fabrizi started New Jersey Fireworks, he must not have been able to use all of the sprawling property that once was Kent Manufacturing, because he subleased some of the property to individuals who started other small firework operations. One of these on the list for Lupoli visits was Brooks Bell, who

You had to start somewhere! Trying to compete with the big boys in the firecracker business was not easy. Standard Fireworks Co., Inc. got their start in one small building.

started Bell Fireworks circa 1963. Brooks Bell must have been quite a character. Brooksy, as he was known, had paid his dues in the firework business. He had also picked up the nickname "Battles" because he was missing part of his arm from an earlier accident and was just generally beat up. Ken relates the story as told to him by Brooksy Bell himself:

> While working in one of the buildings, an aerial shell he was working with somehow ignited. Knowing it was going to be bad, his first reaction was to get the lighted shell outside the building that was full of powder and fireworks to avoid a devastating catastrophe. He ran towards the door with the lighted shell in hand and just barely made it outside when it went off. He saved the day but lost most of is arm in the effort.

There were so many fireworks companies along Fireworks Alley at one time or another that it became a massive jumble as to which was which. The names included Victory (who also manufactured for Hitt's), Spencers, Havre De Grace, Elkton Sparkler, EZ Light Sparkler, Kent, New Jersey, Bell, Keystone, and others that have been lost over time. Ken Lupoli knows why there were so many:

> Whenever a company had an accident, and they all did, it was bad for business, so the owners would wait a few months, clean up the mess, and start again with a new name, usually in the same location.

All of this was happening at the tail end and a little beyond the era of Great American Firecracker. Making fireworks was the only thing these guys knew. They had been in the business all of their lives and now the government was telling them they had to give up their livelihood and quit making fireworks. The critics had finally won with the passing of the Child Protection Act of 1966, successfully putting an end to the legal manufacture of the Great American Firecracker. They had allowed a certain grace period of five years for the industry to make necessary adjustments and sell off any existing stock, but many continued to make firecrackers during this time. What else were they supposed to do when suddenly faced with forced retirement?

The "Boom! Boom!" girls came from all over the country for a good steady job in the munitions plants during World War II and stayed on when the factories converted to making fireworks during peacetime. The average pay in the late 1940s was thirty-eight cents an hour.

The "Boom! Boom!" girls making munitions for the war effort. Although it could be long hours and dangerous work, the women working in the firework factories knew they had a good, dependable job. It was not the type of work you wanted if you were easily spooked!

And all for thirty-eight cents an hour! No doubt this attitude was not too helpful when the big ones came.

In the factories the men generally did the "powder work," which was mixing the various chemicals that made up the formula for what was being made at that time; the women, lots of whom had worked at the factories during the war making munitions, would assemble the goods by hand and pack them in boxes and were affectionately referred to as the "Boom! Boom!" girls.

Most manufacturers did everything they could to improve safety in the workplace, but there were so many safety issues to deal with: a little spilled material, static electricity, storing incompatible finished goods or chemicals in the same place, workers having residue on their clothing or wearing jewelry that would cause a small spark, and dust. Dust (of any kind, not just pyrotechnic materials) when loose in the atmosphere can spontaneously combust, causing a huge explosion; owners of grain elevators have to be particularly aware of this problem. To avoid problems with dust hanging in the air, compositions were often mixed outdoors, or in open and well-ventilated rooms, but then there was the problems climate and weather could produce, such as wind blowing the chemicals or static electricity in the air. It seemed there was always some obstacle to overcome.

What was really scary was the fact that sometimes an explosion could happen for no apparent reason. This was the case of the huge explosion at the Kent plant in 1954, where no one definite cause was ever determined. Usually the main cause of an explosion could be narrowed down to the single most common cause: the mixing of sensitive chemical combinations, chief among these potassium chlorate and sulphur, a very unstable and dangerous mixture that could explode at virtually any time and for any reason. Even small traces of these chemicals on a worker's clothing could cause an explosion. Over time the factories developed completely separate locations for both manufacture and the storage of chlorate and non-chlorate items. Workers who worked with potassium chlorate were not allowed to go to any area of the factory where sulphur or sulphides were being used without first showering and changing clothes. Eventually potassium chlorate would be banned from firework manufacture altogether and replaced by much safer potassium perchlorate.

Firework manufacturing plants were designed and laid out with safety in mind. Generally speaking, the typical operation was spread out over many acres. Where most factories consisted of up to a few buildings, firework factories often had hundreds of buildings scattered over the countryside. There was usually a main administrative building, a few storage warehouses for different types of finished goods (separate warehouses were used for chlorate- based and non-chlorate-based goods), and a warehouse for raw materials and supplies. The bigger factories would sometimes be accessible by railroad. Then there were lots and lots of small shed-type structures where the actual manufacturing was done. These sheds were built in a very specific way. They would have three rather sturdy walls and a sloping roof. The fourth wall, if there was one at all, was located beneath the highest point of the sloping roof and was barely a wall at all. It was built as flimsy as possible, usually consisting of thin sheets of wood or metal loosely held in place. Any doors that were used opened out instead of in. The worker(s) inside would sit at a table upon which the work was placed, positioned so their back faced the wall. The shed was designed and built to fly apart easily if an explosion occurred. By not containing the expanding gases from an explosion the damage and risk of injury could be significantly reduced.

These sheds were then spaced some distance from each other determined by the "blast zone." The blast zone was how far the explosion in one shed could travel and cause the explosion of others in a domino effect. Ken Lupoli relates a story about one of his visits to Tony Fabrizi's place:

My dad and I went to see his buddy, Tony Fabrizi, at the New Jersey plant out on Fireworks Alley one Saturday. We looked all over the property for him until we found him intently working on something in a not-too-sturdy, yet fairly new wooden building. Walking in we found him intent on his work, so intent that we assumed he didn't see a small fire burning in one corner of the building, just under a no smoking sign. I was quite alarmed and pointed this out to him right away.

IT'S ALL FUN AND GAMES UNTIL SOMEONE BLOWS OFF THEIR HANDS!

The anti-firecracker lobby combined real statistics with propaganda to try and get their point across. This National Safety Council poster from the 1930s was meant to shock and scare people away from using firecrackers as they became ever more popular.

"Yeah, I know something's burning over there," he said. "I guess I probably should do something about it 'cause I'm so tired of rebuilding this building. I've had to rebuild it three times in the last five years!" Tony chuckled.

Some of the sheds that were designed to have one blow-away wall were now just three walled structures, the other wall having been blown away sometime earlier.

These guys were so used to the work involved that while being very safety conscious in some aspects, they were completely oblivious in others. Despite all the safety precautions plants exploded all the time: some just little explosions and some major disasters. The firecracker industry was under a lot of pressure by lawmakers trying to ban their products because consumer accidents were mounting. Every year reports would come in about blinded children, blown off fingers, and even death as the result of the use of firecrackers, and the numbers were growing. Add to that the factories themselves were blowing up right and left and it was cause enough for an ever-growing anti-firecracker movement to try and shut them down. But since the jobs were plentiful and the profits high, the firecracker industry fought back, even though they had to know they were providing the public with truly dangerous items—but hey, so was the firearms business! Every July, both before and after Independence day, the anti-firecracker forces would go into full battle mode, demanding legal reform and saturating the newspapers with propaganda mixed with real horror stories.

In June 1936, the National Safety Council reported to the AP some scary statistics. Firecrackers in the hands of little children were still the biggest hazards of the 4th of July holiday. The National Safety Council took on the fireworks industry again, like they did every year, saying that "what the firecracker industry calls 'harmless' caused many accidents and deaths. Firecrackers caused 2,075 of 3,000 accidents studied by the Society for the Prevention of Blindness in 1935." And for that year alone they stated the following statistics: on Independence Day, at least 7,730 persons were injured and thirty killed from fireworks. Nine of those killed and 146 injured were less than five years old. The National Safety Council report goes on to state: "The survey explains that most folks blame high-powered explosives for the accidents they read about. As a matter of fact," the council concludes, "the common firecracker is the real villain." Even sparklers, given to children because of their supposed safety, "caused many injuries and at least two deaths." The study goes on to cite examples typical of accidents caused by firecrackers:

A policeman shattered his hand so badly that amputation was necessary. He was showing a child how to light a firecracker.

A fragment of metal pierced a small boy's heart after he had lit a firecracker under a tin can.

One boy was killed and two passersby were injured after the lad dropped a lighted firecracker into an unused 1,000 gallon gasoline tank that still contained some gas and vapor.

A war veteran who had been cured of shell shock lashed out and shattered his skull against a lamppost. He had been startled by a firecracker thrown at him.

Lighted firecrackers tossed into cars and crowds were found responsible for 1,359 of the 3,000 accidents studied. The report goes on to make recommendations on how to "attack" the problem by passing legislation completely banning all fireworks except those "municipally sponsored and handled by experts to satisfy in a really safe and sane manner the publics appetite for flashing boom booms." Undoubtedly, the National Safety Council was right and most likely presenting factual statements as to the dangerous nature of large firecrackers. Even the manufacturers knew this was true. But they were taking great advantage of the situation by trying to ban the sale of all fireworks. It is easy to see how any of the accidents listed could result in serious injury and even death from the misuse of large firecrackers, but it is not so easy to see how one kills oneself with a sparkler. After all, is a sparkler that much more dangerous than playing with matches in the barn, with grandpa's axe, or a can of gasoline, etc. As the debate heated up several things happened. Many states outlawed the possession of all types of fireworks. Other states approached the problem in a more sensible way with what they called "Safe & Sane" fireworks, outlawing what they determined to be dangerous fireworks but allowing the sales of more tame types so the public could still enjoy their celebrations. Ironically, some of the states that had the nation's largest fireworks plants outlawed their use. The manufacturers countered by exploiting loopholes in state laws. They ramped up mail order sales to "dry" states and produced beautiful catalogs many a young man would stare at for hours and hours until ultimately placing an order and checking the mail anxiously every day for their arrival. They would also create new devices that would exploit the line between what was defined as "Safe and Sane" and what was not. If the consumer wanted fireworks, he could get them regardless of the law. It was increasingly obvious and inevitable that something had to be done about the problem posed by the Great American Firecracker. Americans could not be allowed to run wild in the streets wielding five-inch firecrackers in one hand and a flask of whiskey in the other. The mayor of Elyria, Ohio, posted a warning to his citizens that gave some humorous insight into what was going on:

and to fire it in the streets of Elyria must be considered extremely dangerous. The firing of large firecrackers on the streets and alleys will therefore be considered a violation of the ordinance covering such matters, and person, so offending will be promptly arrested and prosecuted. The firing of large firecrackers on private property will not be interfered with by the police.
—P. D. Reefy, Mayor of Elyria, Ohio

The promiscuous use of firecrackers and rockets on the Fourth of July has become a source of danger to both life and property. Within recent years the firecracker has grown in size from 2 inches to 12 inches, with a diameter of 2 inches. The explosive force of such a cracker is great

Probably the biggest cause of the American firecracker reaching its final demise was the increasing frequency of plant explosions—disasters that claimed many lives. Since the very beginning of firecracker manufacturing in America there had been plant disasters. There were also many explosions in retail stores, warehouses, private homes, delivery vehicles, and illegal bootleg factories. A whole book could be written on this topic alone. Here are the stories of some of the more famous American factory disasters and some very rare and insightful first-hand accounts from survivors who were there to bear witness to the awesome fury.

Hitt's Firework Factory Explosion of 1921

As mentioned earlier, T. G. Hitt was America's premier innovator of the American firecracker and an all-around pyrotechnic genius. Apparently, he was also one of the most safety conscious of all firework manufacturers. Considering all that he accomplished, the size, extent, and the over-fifty-year duration of his operations, and despite numerous small explosions, it is amazing he only had one major explosion at his American operation in Seattle, Washington, that resulted in a death. Remarkably, the explosion that destroyed the factory

in the fall of 1921 only killed one woman. In 1999, a ninety-year-old resident, John Parker, wrote of his experience as witness to the explosion. At the time of the explosion he was in the seventh grade and was seated in a classroom in a two-story school house. It was afternoon, and as he sat facing the windows he witnessed a huge flash of light, followed seconds later by a bone-shaking roar. The whole building shook and quaked. He was gripped with terror as he saw a gigantic column of smoke rising above the Hitt firework plant.

Amidst the smoke debris shot into the sky and leaves and branches were blown off the trees. He describes how he saw the huge water tank and other various machinery and apparatus blown into the air as if in slow motion. He said, "The water tank had a huge pipe going in and one coming out so that the steam shot out and made it appear like a rocket. It spun out and upwards and over, and then finally fell to earth some distance away." The explosion caused so much chaos in the classroom that the teacher had no choice but to dismiss class, telling the children to go directly home. Children being children, they all immediately rushed to the scene of the explosion. Mr. Parker said that upon his arrival at the scene, "The power of the blast had stripped all the limbs and leaves from a huge maple tree, leaving long stubby limbs. A fireman climbed high up in the tree and, using a pike pole, he was able to retrieve a gingham dress that held the rib cage and spinal column of a body. Later they gathered the parts of a human being and put them in a pile. It was my friend's sister.

She had just opened a barrel of black powder; the rest is anybody's guess as to what caused it to ignite."

The accident caused the town to react. They immediately passed new laws outlawing the manufacture of explosives. This and the fact they no longer had a factory caused Hitt's Firework Company to relocate its operations. Hitt's operations had several more buildings catch fire over the years, but these were always minor and were put out by the fire department. I believe Thomas Hitt understood the fireworks manufacturing process better than any other firework maker in America. It was Hitt that understood the disastrous results of mixing potassium chlorate with sulfur (the single greatest cause of firework manufacturing accidents) very early on. With the invention of his new patented flash powder he only resorted to using chlorate formulas when he could find no other way to produce a given effect. Despite this horrible disaster, Hitt's fireworks, one of the largest in the country, was also one of the safest.

Pennsylvania Fireworks Company Explosion of 1930

On the morning of April 3, 1930, in the town of Devon, Pennsylvania, a huge explosion rocked the entire town and surrounding area. The first explosion was immediately followed by two even more powerful explosions, then by many smaller explosions lasting for about a half hour. Devon, Pennsylvania, is a small suburb about fifteen miles west of Philadelphia and was once the home of the Pennsylvania Fireworks Co. Fires raged in many of the small buildings that were scattered over the ten or so acre property. Firemen from all around the area responded to the fires amidst the thick smoke and continuing intermittent small explosions and debris. The explosions could be heard for miles. Cars and trucks were literally blown off of nearby roads and caught on fire, along with houses and buildings blocks away from the plant, further adding to the firemen's task. The local newspaper describing the scene said it resembled a battlefield, and that "Every bit of vegetation was destroyed, large trees ripped apart, their branches shattered and

torn off. The force of exploding fireworks' awesome power left great holes, like shell craters in the black pockmarked earth. Except for the office and one concrete foundation, there was not a timber projecting more than 2 feet above the ground to indicate where any of the buildings had been." Windows were broken up to half a mile away. Burnt and dismembered bodies littered the scene. Upon investigation, it was determined the disaster was caused by the detonation of thirty kegs of black powder that had just been delivered. What caused the detonation was never determined. When it was all over ten people were dead and scores were injured. Most of the dead and injured were employees of the plant, but two young sisters were killed as they played outside the boundary of the plant. To this day, the Pennsylvania Fireworks disaster of 1930 remains the worst disaster ever in the town of Devon and the surrounding area. The plant was never rebuilt.

The Great Explosion of the Kent Fireworks Co., Chestertown, Maryland, July 16, 1954

The Kent Fireworks Co. explosion occurred on July 16, 1954, around 10:30 a.m., and was one of the worst, and certainly the most infamous in America's history. It was also one of the best documented of all of the great American firework factory disasters.

In July 1954, the Kent Fireworks Co. (or as it was officially known, the Kent Manufacturing Co., Inc., leaving the uninitiated in the dark as to just what exactly they manufactured), in the small community of Elkton, Maryland, was the largest manufacturer of fireworks in the country. They had made a transition to the manufacture of fireworks at the end of the war in 1945. Prior to that, they had made detonators, tracer bullets, and other munitions for the war effort. The president of the company, Phillip G. Miller, was also the mayor of the town of Elkton. The Kent Fireworks Co. was by far the largest employer of the people of Elkton. By all accounts it was a good place to work and paid a very good wage of about forty cents per hour. It could be hot, somewhat dirty, a little monotonous, and most definitely dangerous. Long-time employees knew what to expect most of the time, maybe to the point of complacency. Factory operations ran around the clock and most employees could work as much as they wanted, which the employees liked. It meant they could make more money when they needed to.

In 1954, the Kent manufacturing Co. still had a large contract with the federal government, making millions of M-80 salutes for the military, and were the sole suppliers of these large firecrackers used as gunfire simulators. The government-type M-80s were much more powerful than commercial ones made during this time and had to conform to government specs. In the process of completing part of the M-80 order, it was discovered a large supply of the salutes that were about to be packed had not passed government standard specifications. The powder inside the M-80s was leaking out around where the fuse was inserted into the body of the firecracker, so the government had set up a "fix" station to try and salvage the defective M-80s. According to one of the plant managers after the fact, this was done over the strong objections of Kent Co. managers. The

"fix" station that was set up consisted of a string of light bulbs inside a makeshift tunnel with a conveyor running through it. The M-80s would have a type of glue they called "fuse dope" placed around the fuses at the case where the powder was leaking. The M-80s would then be fed through the tunnel fifteen to twenty at a time and the light bulbs would dry the fuse dope; they would then be repacked as they exited the tunnel, fifty to a box. The boxes were packed in wax paper to keep out moisture and then twenty boxes were packed into wooden packing cases. During this process they had accumulated about seventy-five cases of the M-80s.

On September 4, 2009, the Kent County Historical Society in Chestertown, Maryland, held a public meeting at the Emmanuel church. Invited to speak were all the surviving employees and townspeople who remembered that day. That incident left as great an impression as the 9/11/2001 terrorist attacks left on America. This would probably be the last time these people would have the opportunity to have their story heard. Of all the people to testify as to their experiences that day, Maynard Porter's testimony was probably the most informative. Maynard had been the manager of B building, as it was known, and was in the center of the happenings that day. His recollections from over sixty years ago remain vivid and unclouded. He says the scene from that day has replayed every day of his life with the same intensity as the moment it occurred. Here is an edited transcript of Maynard Porter's testimony given on September 4, 2009, in his own words:

Maynard Porter: "The government manufactured these M-80s and none of them passed because they leaked a little bit around the fuse and what we did was to set this up, the government set this up... I objected to the set up, but Mr. Walmer said there was nothing I could do about it. What it was, powder would come out around the fuse and what they had set up was a string of lights. . . turn around and put fuse dope around the fuse to keep it from leaking powder and then they went through the tunnel and it's what went off at first… in the tunnel at any one time was only about 10 or 15 and they would come out the other side and we would repack them. And that's what the first explosion was, and then we had a second explosion. What happened in the second explosion was they had all been repacked in wooden cases, in the wooden cases was 20 boxes, 50 in a box, that box was wrapped in wax-filled paper and inside the box was another waterproof paper to seal all that off so nothing would get into it. What happened was, when the first blow went off, there was a period of time, there was about 50 or 60 cases that was packed ready for shipment and they went, and see, that's what the big explosion was. Now what caused the detonation of anything else, nobody knows. If you're setting someplace with rock strata across it, it goes by the rock strata and another explosion could go off at the other end. But when they got through and checked everything, there was no rock strata in all of this. Why those 50, 75 cases detonated all at one time, there is no answer to it. The government checked everything according to all explosions, but what caused it – what caused the damage, they never figured it out."

"At the start of the explosion, I was just a little ways in the building when the first explosion went off, and I started running out of the building. One of the women came running out of my building and I grabbed her hand, and I was back in the boiler room which was at the back of the building when the whole place detonated. But what they had set up wasn't safe and they knew that, but why those 50 to 75 cases detonated, nothing has ever been proven from that day. According to all, they were inside wooden cases, twice sealed in waterproof paper, so there never was an answer. The government had all those inspectors come in to look at rock strata but they could not find what caused that to go. The last explosion was tremendous. Because you take 50, 75 cases and there's 500 M-80's in a case, why they all detonated at one time, we don't know whatsoever what would cause that type of explosion. "

"The first explosion was a bad set up – nothing justified the government to do it that way so,

that's the whole thing, but what caused the second explosion in the period in between, there's never been an answer to it whatsoever. Because the first thing was to check the rock strata… but there was never no answer to it. The government never could figure out what happened and what caused everything to detonate at one time. The small explosion was here and about 50 feet away was the second explosion and that's what caused the terrific explosion."

Question. "How much time between the two explosions?"

Porter: "I would say it was 4 or 5 minutes because what it was, was I gave the lady to my father-in-law and I had run back to the boiler room when the second explosion happened, so it was just a few minutes in between. But as I say, they could never figure out why the second explosion happened, because according to all history about explosions, if one explosion goes down to rock strata it could travel on rock strata and caused an explosion somewhere else, but there was never no answer to it whatsoever what caused the second explosion."

Previously, at another public meeting on the subject of Elkton's great explosion of 1954, Maynard Porter had given testimony relating to this and other accidents he had experienced during his lifetime of work in the fireworks industry. His comments give some insight into the operations of the factories and how common some of the accidents were in those days:

Porter: "We had a contract from the Triumph Company in Elkton. In the late '20s they made fireworks in Chestertown on the property where the Saltana shipyard is today. They were making two-inch salutes and they blew up. I remember a lot of us boys used to steal them and set them off. We just couldn't stand not having some. Under the railroad tracks there was a place where would set them off. We were kind of wild," he adds with a grin.

"I recall the devastating blast that took 11 lives and seriously injured so many who worked at the plant, which was not the first one in the Chestertown facility suffered. Safety glass blew out – Dr. Dick treated cuts on my face."

"Once the fire also burned down one of the buildings, but did not cause any injuries to workers at the time. It burned down building 188. We had a lot of hand grenade fuses ready to ship. Mr. Wilmer warned the fire company to stay away because they'd blow up 188. But I took them down to the dump and all they did was pop. Some of them lasted about two months in the bottom of the dump, they just kept on popping."

"I would work for hours on Sunday, 24 hours on Monday, and 16 hours the rest of the week. Mr. Wilmer gave me permission to work anytime I wanted to, and I wanted to work as much as I could. The girl who gave out checks was telling everyone how big mine was, and from then on Mr. Wilmer kept it in his drawer. There wasn't any limit to how long you could work every day back then."

"We got a contract to make a bomb nose from Lionel train Corporation in New Jersey. We also continued to make hand grenade fuses in another building after the first one burn."

"I caught one woman who was staggering towards me. I ran back to my building and the whole thing blew up. I was running from the building where the explosion began."

"I got blamed for what happened, but that job was set up the way the government inspectors wanted. I didn't like it. The only thing that saved my life was running out to help the woman staggering out of the building."

"There were two explosions. I won't ever understand how that big bunch of boxes blew, when they were so well sealed. Everyone who got killed was in building B. Some had gotten out of the building, but weren't far enough away."

"I tried to identify the people outside, and I had to decide what door they came out of to know who they were. There was a door off each line so if anything happened they could get out. When they took all the bodies to the armory I tried to identify them again."

"One building went up, then the warehouse just off from that building. A and C buildings were still up. Whistle powder all over the table of one building blew a drum so hard it tore

through the side of that building. But azite powder in another building never went off. The explosion blew out windows with a tremendous amount of concussion, all the way to Steph Manor several miles away. Five people never could be identified."

"I went to the doctor and he gave me medicine to calm my nerves. I lived in rock Hall at the time. I ran the car into the ditch you took a man's mailbox out from between two trees. It calmed me a little too much. The doctor said he meant to tell me I could doze off so be careful after I took medicine. "

"There was a cave with tetryl in it near where the building blew, and if the explosion traveled and reached that, the whole town could have gone up."

"People were running everywhere. Even across the Chester River bridge, and they weren't allowed to come back."

"They could have been forced to rebuild because they had a government contract, but will but Mr. Walmer talked them out of it. One man said it was the dumbest thing that ever happened, because it has been such a successful business and gave a lot of people jobs. It was not the first disaster. There'd been two other explosions at that plant before. We had two blows before the big one. Eisenhower came into Chestertown to speak at Washington College. That day the plant blew up and killed a man. I went over to stop people from coming into the hole in that fence. I stopped them and told them they couldn't come in and found out they were Secret Service men trying to find out the source of the explosion."

Between the years 1929 and 1954, there were six major firework factory disasters in the country's main firework making locations in Maryland and Pennsylvania, and countless other minor explosions that were never even reported. Employees were reluctant to report any small accidents to the authorities. Having been advised by their bosses, they knew their livelihood may be at stake. It is possible that many if not most of these accidents could have been prevented if the employees had not been afraid to speak up if and when they saw violations.

Chapter 8

Great American Firecracker Tales

For all the trouble, destruction, injury, and chaos American firecrackers may have caused, they sure were fun! The power, danger, and the illegality of the dreaded nuisances only made them that much more thrilling to young boys. There were so many things you could do with them, limited only by your imagination.

There are probably only two groups of people that liked cherry bombs more than teen-aged boys: toilet manufacturers and plumbers! After all, that was their job security. With the advent of the waterproof cherry bomb came the destruction of thousands of toilets across America. I don't know what it was about the combination of a toilet bowl and a cherry bomb, but the two seemed to irresistibly go together. And oh boy, would a cherry bomb do a number on a toilet bowl: just light, toss in, and run. Or for even more destruction you could flush it! The water and white porcelain would fly in all directions like some kind of giant ceramic water balloon, and the water would flow like a rushing river until a plumber could be located to shut it off, causing flooded floors and pandemonium! This chaotic scene was repeated in hundreds of high schools and teen dances across America in the 1950s, so much so that it became somewhat of a trademark for the juvenile delinquent

In an attempt to clean up their image and combat the anti-fireworks movement firecracker manufacturers came up with their own propaganda depicting fireworks as what all red-blooded American families did together on America's birthday.

and was even brought before a Senate sub-committee trying to solve the problem of juvenile delinquency. When you thought of a 1950s hoodlum, you thought of a leather jacket, greased back hair, a switchblade knife, and cherry bombs. There was no respectable hoodlum who had not trashed a toilet with a cherry bomb at some time. To this day, if you ask somebody that grew up in the '50s to do a word association and you give them the word "cherry bomb," nine times out of ten they will respond "toilet bowl." The toilet may have been the number one target for the bad boys, but if you were a good kid and had been taught better than to destroy someone else's property, you discovered there were so many more things you could do with a cherry bomb.

Firecrackers were a rite of passage for teenage boys growing up in the 1950s. By then, firecrackers were only legal in a handful of states and you could no longer buy the big cannon crackers of the 1940s. Torpedoes were also illegal, although you could still buy "cracker balls." The only thing still available in the good old USA was the salutes, with cherry bombs being the most popular. There were also silver salutes and M-80s. By

the 1950s, most states had long since passed "Safe and Sane" laws. Living in a safe and sane state did not mean you could not get firecrackers, it just meant they would be very hard to get unless you went out of state, and you had to be very careful not to get arrested. Some states had severe penalties for sales and possession of illegal fireworks, and my home state of Indiana was one of them.

My first experiences with firecrackers started when I was about eight years old. I traded with my best friend Bert, who had just come back from vacation with a prize. Behold! A whole brick of Black Cat firecrackers, wrapped in beautiful red cellophane, with that familiar picture of a mean black cat's face on the label. Thirty-two firecrackers in a pack and forty packs in the brick! Wow! I had never seen this before and I was immediately hooked. I wanted some bad. But Bert knew he had a great treasure in his possession and he was very shrewd. He stored his prize under his bed, and every time we

A young boy with his arms already full of 4th of July treasures gazes longingly at the stacks of firecrackers and cap guns in the local sporting goods store display window, c. 1950.

were together at his house, he would get it out and we would look at it. He would let me hold it and admire it. Bert would have made a great poker player; he was slow and deliberate in the execution of his master plan. I, being the impetuous sort, would probably have had that brick ripped open as soon as we left the store with it, but he didn't even open it for more than a whole month, just fondling it and showing it off. He had been doing the same thing to all his other "pals" in our neighborhood, until he had us all where he wanted us. Finally one day, our neighborhood gang was altogether in Bert's back yard. Bert emerged from his back door with the Black Cat brick in hand, sat down on the porch steps, and began to unwrap the bundle, first slowly and carefully peeling the label from the front of the brick, cursing when a small piece of the label tore and remained attached to the red cellophane. We all gathered round as he repeated this process with the red cellophane wrapper and all forty packs spilled out onto the steps. Bert then picked up the packs and neatly stacked them

in a shoebox he had saved especially for that purpose; he packed all but one pack and put the lid back on the box. With the same slow care and diligence he opened the pack of firecrackers as we all huddled ever closer to see the goods. Bert then started to unbraid the naked string of firecrackers and two fell loose at his feet. He placed the rest back in the shoebox, reached into his pocket, pulled out a Zippo lighter, and carefully lit the fuse. We all scurried to make room for him to throw the firecracker onto the lawn. BANG! He held the other firecracker up for all to see and then lit it. BANG! And so the negotiations began in earnest! What would you trade for your first unopened pack of thirty-two Black Cat firecrackers? Remember what I said, once you smell black powder you are forever hooked, and I was. I finally gave up about a dozen comic books, two *Mad* magazines, and a completed model of Frankenstein for a single pack. Seeing how I was Bert's best friend, I later learned I had gotten a much better deal than the rest of the neighborhood kids. The transactions lasted about a full

Young children try to get the deposit back for a couple Nehi bottles in hopes of buying a box of sparklers for the 4th of July picnic in the park.

Early in the morning, children decorate the family business for a 4th of July parade down main street. The holiday was usually jam packed with parades, contests, picnics, and of course, lighting firecrackers.

In "safe and sane" states such as Indiana, the most a boy could hope for to celebrate the 4th with some noise was a trusty cap gun. Here a boy stands in a cloud of smoke getting an early start.

gone. I had to have more! It was time for a serious quest.

After that, I managed to get a few packs of firecrackers on my own. Here or there, if I heard some going off somewhere I would drop what I was doing and check it out. I could usually talk somebody into selling me a pack or two. If you could find a place where they had lit a long string of firecrackers there would always be a few that did not go off you could scrounge. Once when my older sister was babysitting me at her and her husband's house, I came across an unopened string of a hundred in their garage. I just could not resist the urge! I opened them up, took a few off the string, and began lighting them behind the garage. I didn't even bother to leave the scene of the crime. I was immediately grabbed by the scruff of my neck by my very angry brother-in-law. He yelled at me, "Those don't belong to you! I was saving those for the 4th of July!" I felt so bad. I explained to him that I was sorry. I wasn't a thief, I just couldn't help myself. He was cool. He told me he understood and we went back to the garage, where he gave me half the string. He was older and wiser, but apparently he had suffered from the same compulsion at one time and he knew where I was coming from. What a guy!

I got older and was able to ride my bike wherever I liked, and with the approaching 4th of July holiday, word spread there was a shady character from out of state that had set up a safe and sane fireworks stand on the highway a few miles from my house. Bert and I would ride our bikes up and hang out on the busy corner by his stand and talk to him about fireworks. After a while, I observed he was hauling his fireworks to the stand in a beat up old Ford station wagon…with Tennessee plates! "Ding! Ding! Ding! Bert, tell him what he has won!" Tennessee, see…one

month until half the brick was traded off, at which time Bert suspended the trading. He had made quite the haul and still had half a brick of firecrackers left, but I was satisfied with the deal.

You would have thought I had acquired a bar of gold! That pack of thirty-two firecrackers lasted about a year. I kept them in a cigar box under my bed and would take them out and look at them almost every day. It would have to be a very special day for me to actually light one, savoring them one at a time until they were all

Young boys with their cap guns, awake since before sunrise on the 4th of July and waiting for the proprietor of a sporting goods store to arrive and open the store.

of the legal firecracker states! I had a strong hunch that the sparklers, snakes, and fountains he had so neatly on display were not the only thing this guy was peddling. Who in their right mind would come all the way to Indiana from Tennessee just to sit out in the summer sun all day long and sell a few boxes of sparklers at ten cents a box? What's wrong with this picture? Bert and I immediately worked on him. We begged and pleaded to buy some firecrackers, but he would not budge. "All I have is safe and sane!" he insisted. We knew that selling firecrackers to a minor was a serious violation with a hefty fine. The local fire marshal was telling everybody that on the television, chanting it night after night like some kind of mantra. The guy was obviously afraid he would get busted, so we decided to just wait him out. We would hang out most of the day or go and come back and hound him to death, but it was not working. He would not budge. Maybe he wasn't lying and all he had was safe and sane. Then we got a lucky break, just as we were about to give up. We rode our bike up to his stand first thing in the morning for the third day in a row. We arrived just in time to see him closing the tailgate on his station wagon and standing next to him was a customer, an older man with a big brown paper bag. We cruised right up to where they were both standing and then and there I decided to go for broke. I told the guy from Tennessee in no uncertain terms that the jig was up. We were wise to what he was doing. He had a choice: either sell us some firecrackers or we were going to rat him out to the cops. He finally relented and he opened the side door of the station wagon. It was

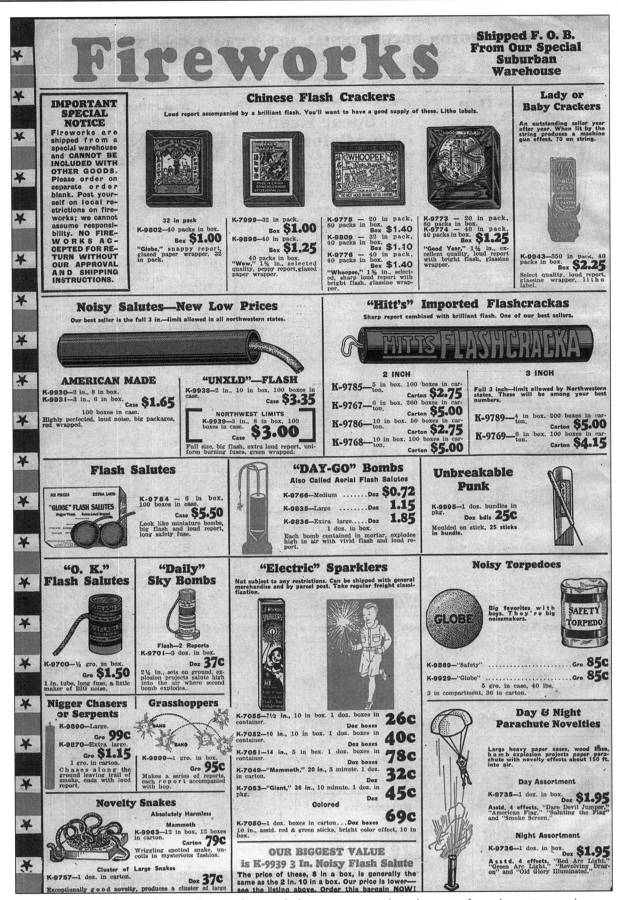

For a short while, firecracker retailers tried to reach the vast untapped market in "safe and sane" states by offering their goods via mail order. Most states were quick to close that loophole.

not what I expected to see. He had removed all of the back seats and covered the back windows with brown paper. There were some food wrappers and a couple sleeping bags, that was it. We figured poor sap, he must be living in his wagon and trying to eek out a living. But before we could burst into tears of sympathy, he threw back one of the sleeping bags, revealing all manor of skyrockets and roman candles. Whoosh! He threw back the other sleeping bag, revealing bricks of firecrackers of all different brands and colors. I knew it! "OK, what do you want?" he asked. "Cherry bombs!" Bert blurted out. It was about time we had some of the good stuff. Up until now all we had ever had was Chinese inch-and-a-half firecrackers. But I didn't see any cherry bombs or large salutes. The guy walked around to the rear of the wagon and lifted up two boxes of rockets or something, uncovering a hatch. He lifted it open and lo and behold, maybe fifty boxes of big salutes. Cherry bombs, silver salutes, you name it. And boy oh boy was he nervous! "Make it snappy," he barked, but we just wanted to soak it all in. After a few seconds he threatened to shut the door, so we scrambled to make our choices. Bert got a half gross of silver salutes and some bottle rockets, I got a half gross of cherry bombs, and we split a brick of Atomic Firecrackers. We spent every cent we had earned mowing lawns. I don't recall how much we spent, but the prices were through the roof. He shoved our purchases into brown paper bags just about as fast as a human being can move and slammed the door. He was none too happy, even though he had just taken every cent we had, and wasn't that the reason he had driven all the way from Tennessee and risked arrest? "Now scram kiddies," he exclaimed. Bert and I discussed this guy's ungrateful rudeness and how we felt like we had been treated as second-class citizens as we stowed our goods for the long ride home. I noticed Bert fumbling with his salute box and assumed he was making sure he got what he had paid for. As we started to pedal away Bert suddenly turned around. I saw his hands leave the handle bars as he made a large sweeping circle with his bike and I saw the trail of smoke and sparks fly through the air. In what was a perfectly executed series of moves worthy of the ballet, Bert had lit and thrown a salute while turning a circle with no hands on his bike. The salute landed with pinpoint accuracy in the gutter of the four-lane highway and about ten feet in front of the vendor's stand. KER-POW! As we gained speed on our bikes down that side road, we could hear

the vendor cursing as he tried to chase us down. I might have felt bad about it, but he was such a jerk.

From that point on, Chinese firecrackers were not that hard to come by; you just had to have connections, which I had established. But the anti-firecracker lobby was making it harder and harder to get Cherry Bombs, M-80s, and Silver Salutes. By 1965, it was obvious the anti-firecracker lobby was going to win. The manufacturers were putting up a good fight and tying things up in the courts, but with injuries and outrage mounting, it was inevitable they would eventually be banned forever. And teenaged boys and college students were not helping the cause one bit with our antics. In August 1966, Congress passed the Child Protection Act, but the legislation left open a couple loopholes, including allowing retailers and manufacturers five years to get rid of their old stock, as previously discussed. Second, they allowed an exemption for farmers and the agricultural industry to continue using firecrackers under the guise of pest control. Farmers used various types of firecrackers and salutes to scare birds away from their crops close to harvest time. The salutes would be tied onto a slow-burning rope fuse in a long string, creating an adjustable way to time the ignition of the salutes. They were usually timed so that a salute would explode about every fifteen minutes, scaring away pesky birds that were eating crops. They set this all up on an honor system of sorts. The people selling them were supposed to be making sure that anybody who should not have them did not get them. All you really needed to buy salutes after the law went into effect was to sign a simple form saying you were a farmer and were going to use the salutes for pest control.

In typical government fashion, the bureaucracy made a mess out of the new law. First, the passing of the law increased demand for firecrackers. People who wanted them knew they would soon not be able to get them anymore, so they stocked up. Second, the supply wasn't really decreasing anytime soon because the manufacturers were really still making them and had no plans to stop without being forced to do so. This created an illusion of limited supply and high demand that made prices skyrocket, with big profits for the makers and retailers. And all that was really needed to still purchase them was a simple form. Everybody knew it couldn't last forever and were making one last grab at it for old time sake.

This opened one last window of opportunity for my friends and I and we went for it. In 1965, my best friend Bert got his driver's license. He was a couple years older than me, so this started to cause a drift between us. After all, he could now date girls and that was way more fun than hanging around with the guys. I got it. But that summer, with the 4th of July just around the corner, we could finally take a trip out of state and get some cherry bombs, so for a month or two we all mowed lawns, washed cars, ran errands, and saved every penny for our big trip to Ohio. In late June, we set out on our trip across the width of Indiana, across the border and about fifty miles into Ohio. Somebody had given us a specific address in an industrial area. We expected to see a regular firework stand, but when we arrived at the address, what we found was a generic-looking warehouse with a single unmarked door. Walking in, you would have thought you were in an auto parts warehouse. There was just a small counter with no sign of fireworks anywhere. But we were prepared. Others had told us about the procedure, so in walked the three of us and we all bellied up to the counter. The man behind the counter asked if he could help us. "Yes sir, the three of us are farmers and we are here to buy some 'pest control devices' for our cornfields. The man scrutinized us closely, enjoying watching us squirm. "So you boys are farmers, are you?" he asked. I'm sure he had seen a couple hundred fifteen-year-old farmers just that week! "Sure we are!" we replied. He asked us a few more questions and small talk before he eventually pulled out clip boards and made us fill out forms of release saying that we were indeed farmers and that we would not hold their company liable for any mishaps. "Oh, don't you worry about that date of birth box, just leave that blank" he said (wink, wink). With that out of the way, he went into the back and brought out three perfectly square boxes. Gone was all the beautiful patriotic artwork on the boxes we had seen before. Rather, they were all covered over with stickers with paragraphs of federal regulations and stamped "for pest control only." He set them on the counter and opened the lids: the first was Silver Salutes, the second contained Cherry Bombs, and the last had red tubes marked M-80, all half-gross boxes. He said "this is what we have, $25

a box and a limit of 4 boxes." I was not prepared for the cost, but obviously he knew he had a dying gold mine. I had exactly $65. I thought it just might be worth a shot, so I made an offer of $65 for a box of each and he accepted. On the way back I wondered if he would have accepted $50, as the others ate hot dogs and drank Coca-Colas I could not afford. We pulled back the rubber mat that lined the trunk of Bert's 1962 Studebaker Lark and tried as best we could to hide ten half-gross boxes of salutes there for the long and scary ride back home. We imagined what criminals we had become and how long we might spend in jail if caught on the wrong side of the state line with all that explosive power. The ride back was wonderful for being so uneventful. We were so excited and all we could think about was all the creative ways we could use our newly acquired firecrackers. The quest we had so long anticipated had gone so smoothly and had finally become a reality. Mission accomplished! Once we were safely home with the goods, I took my three boxes straight to the garage and one by one dumped the contents of each box on the workbench to admire and count. Damn! Each half-gross box (seventy-two pieces) contained only 67 pieces. Five short! What a racket! No wonder he hadn't minded giving me a price break! Given the nature of their customers, they probably thought nobody would complain, and they were right. I was as happy as could be! I could sell off one box and pay for the other two and still have money left over for my next purchase. As soon as I could, I sent away to the Johnson Smith Co. for a deluxe model "Wrist Rocket" slingshot. A wrist rocket and a Cherry Bomb seemed to be made for each other. Was I the only one to make this discovery? I could crawl out the window of my second story bedroom, climb up a makeshift ladder, and gain access to the second story roof. Since most of the houses in the neighborhood were only one story, I could see almost every house from my watchtower position. From this place, I could skillfully place a lighted cherry bomb in any neighborhood yard within about a one-block radius and be back inside, looking out the window, before it went off! Then watch the cops, if they arrived, try to figure out from whence it came.

M-80 Fishing

Another favorite summer past time of ours was fishing. Not the boring way with a hook and a pole; I didn't have patience for that when I was a kid. No, the way to fish was with a waterproof M-80 or cherry bomb that would actually go off underwater. We had a lagoon very near our house where we spent most of our summer vacation. A half an hour's walk through the woods would get you to our secret swimming hole that nobody knew about. We went there almost everyday, skinny dipping, smoking cigarettes, swinging from the rope swing, and catching frogs. It was here that we mastered the skills needed for M-80 fishing. To be successful conditions had to be just right. The waters had to be still and not choppy and there had to be some decent-size fish close to the shore that you could see. Sometimes we would wade out a little bit and stand there and wait. You had to have your fish catcher prepared ahead of time, but it was easy if you knew how. First you would find the right rock; it was best to find one that was flat so that if you threw it in the water just right it didn't have a lot of surface area that would make a big splash. Then you securely attached an M-80 to the rock using either a rubber band or tape. Now came the tricky part. You had to figure out the situation and make a plan on just how to deliver the knock out punch. It all depended on the lay of the land and the disposition of the fish. If you had already caused a lot of disturbance in the water and had not scared the fish away, chances are they had become accustomed to it. It this case slipping the bomb in the water would not scare them off. You could throw the bomb in a little past their position compared to the shore. When the bomb went off it would send a powerful shock wave through the water, knocking all the fish out in about a five-foot radius. You had about thirty seconds to pick them out of the water before they came to again. If you could manage to slip one of these in a school of fish, you could catch several at one time. There have been times when the big fish are so hungry, they will come right up to an M-80 floating on the surface (no rock), thinking it is food and ka-boom, knocked out cold with a huge splash to boot.

Scouts

Another tale of mischief with fireworks happened when I was about thirteen years old and was in the Boy Scouts, only this time the joke was on me.

Every so often the Boy Scouts would have these huge events called Jamborees. Thousands of Scouts with different troops from all over the state would converge on the large Boy Scout camp for a week-long camp out that would end with an awards ceremony held in an amphitheater-style arena that held several hundred people. In the very center of the arena they had built the makings of the biggest bon fire you will ever seen. The pile of wood for that fire must have stood two stories tall. The idea was that at the start of the awards program, having previously added a little accelerant to the bon fire, a person dressed as a Native American would appear at the top of the arena rim and shoot a flaming arrow into the base of the woodpile, thus lighting the bon fire and starting the ceremony. Then the Native American would come down and be joined by others who would dance around the campfire a bit, then spread out into the audience of Boy Scouts, picking out all of the scouts that were to receive an award that night and bring them down to the arena floor for the awards ceremony. I loved the Boy Scouts and was very proud of the fact that I had been chosen by my troop to receive the prestigious Order of the Arrow award. Little did I know that somebody in my troop thought he should have the award instead of me and thought it would be a great idea to load the campfire with firecrackers. The night before the day of the ceremony, after all of the bon fire wood had already been perfectly stacked, the jealous scout and his buddy filled a brown paper grocery bag with several hundred Chinese firecrackers and a handful of cherry bombs and snuck down to the arena, strategically placing it high up in the center of the bon fire stack, trying to assure the fire would reach it at the most opportune time in the ceremony.

So at sundown the ceremony commenced. I was already a nervous wreck because part of the award that I was winning required that I go off into the woods by myself and stay there overnight. Also I was not allowed to utter a single word to anybody once the Native American had picked me out. Some award, huh? But it really was an honor.

Everything went as planned: the Native American appeared, shot the arrow, and the campfire slowly came to life. The ceremonial dance around the bon fire took place, and then the Native Americans dispersed into the crowd to find the award recipients, of which there may have been twenty-five. A Native American approached me from the front, looked me in the eye, gave me three sharp blows to the top of my shoulders, and picked me up. I followed him down to the arena floor. They made a circle of all the award winners around the circumference of the arena floor and took another couple laps dancing around the campfire, then stopped with one Native American behind each scout. The scout leader who was to give out the individual awards was announced and took his place at the podium and the crowd applauded. KA-POW! KA-POW! KA-POW! All hell broke loose! The explosions caught everybody by surprise. The concussions from the salutes were hurling flaming campfire embers and sparks in all directions and scouts

and parents were running helter skelter. Nobody knew what was happening. The firecrackers seemed to last forever, though in reality it was probably just a few seconds. My guide and I just stood there in amazement for a while until a blast sent a flaming piece of wood right past my ear. In a short time it was over and by then most people had figured out what happened. Although most people were frightened at being caught by surprise, there was little panic and most people, having been exposed to salutes and firecrackers, figured out what was happening rather quickly. Although this happening caught me completely by surprise, it really shouldn't have. The guy that did it was bunking in the same tent as I was. I had recalled previous signs of his plotting and just hadn't paid attention to what was going on. It didn't take the scoutmaster long to figure out who did it. The next morning I was called into his office. By the time I got there, the culprit had already told his tale. Problem was he had told the scoutmaster I had been in on it from the start. They called both of our parents to come and pick us up and we were tossed out of camp and the boy scouts. I protested the whole thing as being unfair, but my protests were in vain. Because of my known association with firecrackers it was assumed I was guilty. What a shame. I had been had. I loved the Boy Scouts. It took me almost a full year of trying but they finally let me back in, but it was never the same after that summer.

Other Events

Although I was rather mischievous with my firecrackers, I was never malicious or destructive. I can honestly say I never blew up a toilet or threw them at anyone. Well, actually we would just love to throw a cherry bomb behind a group of chattering girls and scare the daylights out of them, but that was just too much fun to resist. I did, however, enjoy blowing things up: watermelons, tomatoes (lots of fruit and vegetables), coffee cans, buckets, and my own toys, especially toy soldiers and model airplanes.

I guess the crew I ran with were all pretty good kids when compared to the deeds of others. I could not believe the things real hoodlums would do with the big

salutes until I read stories in the old newspapers from the 1940s and 1950s. I had always heard stories of some of the depraved things some boys would do with stray animals and cherry bombs, but I tried not to think about that. I have been an animal lover all of my life and I personally never witnessed, nor would I ever tolerate any type of animal cruelty. But whether it was pranks gone bad or serious malicious intent, once I grew up, I had to admit the people who worked so hard to abolish the large firecrackers were right to want them outlawed. It is hard to imagine in today's society people running wild with handfuls of tiny bombs and the general public at the mercy of just what they would do with

By banning the big salutes and giving the firecracker industry five years to sell off their existing stocks the government created more demand and drove prices up. Everybody wanted a stockpile before the ban went into effect.

them. What a scary thought! Yet that is just the way it was. The criminal mind can be very creative in its search for madness and mayhem. Here are a few of the more dastardly things people did with Great American Firecrackers:

Cadillac, Michigan – Police and the fire department were called out shortly after midnight with reports of explosions and breaking glass in the downtown retail district of the city. A gang of hoodlums had been seen taping M-80 firecrackers to more than a dozen large plate glass department store windows. The firecrackers exploded, shattering the windows and setting off burglar alarms, as well as destroying window display fixtures and merchandise. Damages were estimated at more than $50,000.

In rural Illinois, a car full of youths using cherry bombs blew up every mailbox along a section of farm road. More than fifty mailboxes were destroyed in one night. The boys were never caught.

South Bend, Indiana – Sometime after 2 a.m., police started receiving panicked calls from several terrified citizens who were awakened by an explosion coming from their living room or elsewhere inside their house. One newlywed couple, fearing a natural gas leak, had called from their neighbor's house. They ran there in their pajamas and told police they were afraid to return to their house. Because they had received several calls from that general area with the same complaint, police feared a gas leak and called the gas company, then went to investigate. They arrived to find the newlyweds huddled in the front yard of their home. Upon inspection of the couple's home, police found a large scorched area just inside the front door and bits of material they determined to be from a cherry bomb. After investigating several of the other calls in the area, police determined the cause of the problem. The houses in that neighborhood all had a slot in the front door used for mail. Someone was lighting cherry bombs and dropping them through the mail slots in the entry doors. The cherry bombs were exploding inside their homes.

Beloit, Wisconsin - a group of youths were apprehended while trying to blow open the coin storage boxes of a series of pay phone booths. They were arrested and a large quantity of M-80 firecrackers was confiscated.

In a suburb of Cleveland, police responded to calls of explosions at a bank at approximately 1:30 a.m. on a Sunday night. Upon arriving at the bank they found signs of tampering to the door of the night depository.

After summoning the bank president to the scene and opening up, they found that several large firecrackers had been forced into the night depository, blowing much of the weekend's deposits to bits.

Loveland, Ohio - In a bit of a switch, an eighteen-year-old man was shot and killed by an angry homeowner as he and his friends drove around town lighting and throwing cherry bombs out the window of their car. The shooter, who was charged with manslaughter, said he was fed up with the harassment but was merely trying to scare the boys.

Madison, Wisconsin - A sixteen-year-old girl was seriously injured with burns to her face suffered when a snowball fight got out of hand. One of the boys on the opposing side decided to put a cherry bomb inside the snowball he then threw at the girl.

Cherry Grove Beach, SC - Two small boys, forbidden by their mother to buy firecrackers, were caught with the goods when they returned from the grocery store, but they evaded a trip to the woodshed by telling their mother that their cherry bomb was really a smoke bomb for getting rid of mosquitoes. She was satisfied and put the bomb on a kitchen shelf. That night, while cooking supper, she noticed some mosquitoes. She put the smoke bomb on the table, lit it, and casually walked away. The results were a loud BOOM, shattered nerves, one ruined tablecloth, some broken dishes, a box of salt dropped into a pot of peas, and two paddled posteriors… but the mosquitoes were still there!

Three West Texas State University freshmen were fined $100 and placed on one year's probation after being charged with the destruction of US property. They had placed a military M-80 in a sock full of human feces into a postal box. The explosion damaged five postal boxes and made quite a mess.

All things considered, I have concluded it is best to be able to fondly reminisce about the era of the Great American Firecracker, rather than to still be living in it. Making these firecrackers illegal was a good thing and saved many lives. The golden era of the Great American Firecracker was a time of innocence, responsibility, morals, and values that have vanished

from today's American society, and with it went the firecracker. Thankfully, we still have the memories, stories, and the artifacts of this interesting aspect of American history and I sure am glad I was there.

A drop of ink, t'is said,
Made millions think:
A spark of fireworks has oft'
Made thousands blink.

Bibliography

Dotz, Warren, Jack Mingo, George Moyer. *Firecrackers: The art and History*. Berkely, California. Teen Speed Press, 2000.

The Great Explosion. The Historical Society of Kent County, 2009.

Wiengart, George. *The Dictionary and Manual of Fireworks*. New Orleans, LA, 1937

Klofkorn, Warren K. *Bonfires and Illuminations*. Dingman's Ferry, PA. American Fireworks News, 1994

Acknowledgments

Special thanks to Ken Lupoli for his expertise and access to his vast collection. His help was tireless as he told me tales of his childhood, growing up amongst the firecracker legends along infamous Fireworks Alley. Ken's wonderful, entertaining way of telling the stories of his youth made researching this book a lot of fun.

Special thanks to the Historical Society of Cecil County, Maryland, for all their help digging up material on the Triumph Firework Co. for me on a regular basis. You can contact them by email at cecilhistory.org, or better yet, stop in and tell them I sent you.

Special thanks to Virginia H. Wright, Executive Director, Rainier Valley Historical Society, 3710 S. Ferdinand St., Columbia City, PO Box 18143, Seattle, WA, 98118 (206-723-1663) for all the great information on America's firecracker genius, T. G. Hitt.

Special thanks to the Historical Society of Kent County, Maryland, for all their help and materials relating to the Great Explosion of 1954. Email them at KentCountyHistory.org.

A very special thanks to the mysterious Dr. N. Cowen for sharing his vast and unusual collection. His collection rivals any I have seen.

Thanks to Camille for patience, love, and understanding, and also for carrying the weight.

Rest in peace Dooflopy, who passed peacefully in his sleep the day I finished writing. You will be missed but always remembered.

Index

Glossary

Black powder: Gunpowder, an explosive powder used in fireworks and fire arms made from potassium nitrate, sulphur, and charcoal.

Brick: A way of packaging multiple packs of Chinese firecrackers. Usually marked as 16/40, meaning forty packs of sixteen firecrackers are in the brick. Bricks can be all different sizes.

Barrel Bomb: A type of firecracker shaped like a whiskey barrel. Usually the shell of it was made of sawdust and glue.

Cannon Cracker: A very loud firecracker, usually larger than 4 inches by ½ inch long.

Cherry Bomb: A spherical firecracker usually made of sawdust and glue and dyed red with a green fuse. Named because it resembles a cherry.

Composition: A firework formula consisting of the combination of two or more chemicals.

Crackers: Short for most any type of firecracker of any size. Used when talking about salutes, cannon crackers, cherry bombs, or regular firecrackers.

Flashcrackas: The name copyrighted by T. G. Hitt referring to his brand of firecracker made using photo flash powder.

Flashcracker or Flashlight cracker: A type of firecracker that produces a flash of bright light when detonated. Made with photo flash powder rather than black powder.

Flash Powder: Refers to photographic flash powder, a composition containing magnesium or aluminum that produces a brilliant flash of light when ignited.

Fuse: String or paper wrapped gunpowder designed to deliver fire to a device and also act as a time delay, providing time to get away from an explosive device.

Gunpowder: See black powder.

Pyrobilia: Collectible vintage artifacts dealing with fireworks. Can be catalogs, labels, advertisements, live or spent fireworks, or pyro tools and apparatus.

Pyrotechnics, pyrotechnician, or pyrotechnician: Refers to the art and science of fireworks. A person trained in the chemical compositions, formulas, and construction of fireworks and firework materials.

M-80: A large salute-type firecracker originally made for the US military to be used as a gunfire simulator. M stands for Military and 80 stands for the amount of charge it contained, measured in grains.

Salute: An extra-loud firecracker. Firecrackers up to four inches long were called salutes, while firecrackers over four inches were called cannon crackers.

Silver Salute: A regular salute made popular by being wrapped in silver paper.

Torpedoes: Impact firecrackers. Firecrackers that do not have to be lit, but are detonated by being thrown down on a hard surface.

Jack Nash is a musician, artist, and writer. He began collecting firework labels at a very early age, and eventually became a licensed pyrotechnician. Active in the entertainment field, Jack developed special indoor pyrotechnic effects for the stage. He has done custom artwork for celebrities including Tim Robbins, Jason Priestly, and Teller.